Praise for the Innovative Leadership V for Emerging Leaders and Managers

Part of a larger series that addresses various stages of development throughout one's career, the Innovative Leadership Workbook for Emerging Leaders and Managers lays out a process for individuals, early in their career to think about their development in the context of the organizational culture and systems. It also provides a host of tools to address different needs—a critical success factor for attracting and retaining talent in varying career stages in an organization.

Kate Terrell, Vice President, Human Resources
Global Products Organization, Whirlpool Corporation

■■■■■■

With the raging war for talent, organizations are looking for straightforward, easily accessible ways to develop their existing workforce. HR organizations will be pleased to find this workbook flexible enough to be used by aspiring leaders independently or as part of a comprehensive leader development program. If you're new to the challenges of leadership or have been figuring it out on your own, this workbook will guide you every step of the way!

Michelle Reese, Associate Vice President, HR Strategy, Communications,
and Change Management, The Ohio State University

■■■■■■

Great leaders acknowledge the need for constant growth and development. The concepts in this workbook provide a framework that supports this development while emphasizing the particular needs of an emerging leader. Through the use of this workbook, you will be able to define your own strengths as a leader and gain important insight into how to use those leadership capacities to influence others, create a vision, and to make a positive contribution to an organization.

Amy Barnes, Ph.D., Faculty, The Ohio State University

■■■■■■

Strong technical skills are the foundation of a great engineer. Just as engineers, the most successful leaders best augment these skills with self-awareness, authenticity, an ability to manage multiple highly complex issues, and an ability to navigate organizational politics with finesse. This workbook helps strong performers build on those skills to become either stronger individual contributors or highly effective leaders.

Ahmet Selamet, Chair, Department of Mechanical and Aerospace Engineering,
The Ohio State University

■■■■■■

This workbook helps you ask key questions of yourself as you emerge into leadership roles. Be patient as you grow. Take notes and be grateful for both good and mediocre leaders. The good ones model the way. The bad ones remind us what not to do. This workbook will help shape you into an "excellent" leader.

Carla Paonessa, Chair, LeaderShape Board of Directors
and Retired Managing Partner, Accenture

As a recent college graduate, I had been looking for opportunities to further my development as a leader. The Innovative Leadership Workbook for Emerging Leaders and Managers has helped me to build invaluable skills to support moving into a new entrepreneurial role. The exercises help me understand my strengths and determine my developmental goals. The workbook and exercises have shaped my approach to life, both personally and professionally.

**Anna Klatt, Entrepreneur, Mindful Management, LLC.,
LeaderShape Institute Graduate**

■■■■■■

Maureen and her co-authors have put together a fantastic workbook for young leaders that provides ways to apply leadership theory in a structure that makes sense. The examples of the vision-based exercises will be useful for anyone looking for a foundation on which to begin.

Roger Chen, Google Analyst, LeaderShape Institute Graduate

■■■■■■

In today's dynamic world, it is critical for organizations to create a leadership development pipeline that will enhance its ability to create distance and differentiation from the competition. Leaders need solid skills to be prepared to meet the growing complexity of problems they are facing on a daily basis. This workbook affords organizations the opportunity to develop leaders using a self-paced approach that can augment internal or external development programs.

Michael Linton, Retired CEO Adecco, CEO Staffing Leadership

■■■■■■

A seasoned mentor will guide you through the early stages of your development as a leader. For those of you who don't have that mentor, there's Innovative Leadership for Emerging Leaders and Managers. Guided by this book, you'll develop your understanding, testing, and learning about your own leadership.

**Jim Ritchie-Dunham, President of the Institute for Strategic Clarity and
Adjunct Faculty, EGADE Business School, Harvard**

INNOVATIVE LEADERSHIP WORKBOOK FOR EMERGING LEADERS AND MANAGERS

Field-Tested Processes and Worksheets for Innovating Leadership, Creating Sustainability, and Transforming Organizations

MAUREEN METCALF

WORKBOOK SERIES EDITOR: MARK PALMER

First Published by
Integral Publishers
1418 N. Jefferson Ave.
Tucson, AZ 85712

Published in the United States with printing and
distribution in the United Kingdom, Australia, and
the European Union.

ISBN: 978-1-4675-2280-9

First Printing November 2012

Cover Design, Graphics and Layout by
Creative Spot - www.creativespot.com

Acknowledgments

Contributing Authors: Belinda Gore, Ph.D., Demetrius D. Jackson, Jason Miller, Mike Morrow-Fox, Jonathan Naber, and Mark Palmer.

The theoretical giants on whose hard work we built the Innovative Leadership Fieldbook model: Terri O'Fallon, Ph.D., Susanne Cook-Greuter, Ph.D., Hilke Richmer, Ed.D., Roxanne Howe-Murphy, Ed.D., Peter Senge, Ph.D., Cindy Wigglesworth, Ph.D., and Ken Wilber, M.A., who not only shared their theories, but whose ongoing guidance and encouragement helped us to create a solid framework that is comprehensive and theoretically grounded.

Our friends and colleagues who served as constant cheerleaders and occasional editors, listened to our stories and dreams about the book, and helped us make it come to fruition. Carla Morelli and Michelle Reese offered particularly insightful feedback.

Our teachers, trainers, and mentors, who taught us how to lead—and when to follow.

Our clients who participated as case studies, as well as MBA students who gave feedback on the book by virtue of doing graduate work using the Fieldbook that served as the foundation for this workbook.

Our families who inspired us to be thoughtful and dedicated to our work, and to contribute to the world in a meaningful way.

Our publisher and friend, Russ Volckmann, Ph.D.

Graphic design and layout firm Creative Spot, copy editor Sara Phelps, as well as editors, reviewers, endorsers, thought partners, and countless others who spent untold hours making this possible.

Table of Contents

FOREWORD

"Leadership is a choice." - Warren Bennis

This quote by Warren Bennis, widely known as a leadership author and leader in higher education, is my favorite. Hands down. It is simple, eloquent, easy to remember. And right. Clearly, this is my opinion, but as someone who has read and heard numerous quotes on leadership throughout my life, I keep coming back to this.

We have many choices to make in our lives. We can choose our career, our partner, our attitude, our dinner option, but perhaps there is no more important choice to make in our lives than how we are going to make a difference with the limited time we have on this planet. Far too many of us *choose* to live lives of insignificance and mediocrity because we don't see ourselves as leaders, or as even having the capability to make a difference in our communities much less our own lives. So we bounce from day to day without purpose or passion.

I have used this quote from Bennis quite often in my work leading a not-for-profit organization in an attempt to de-mystify the concept of leading. In attempts to define it, we have made leading far too complicated. I have been keeping a list of all the books on leadership that have thrown another adjective in front of "leadership" to sell their version of it. *Ultimate* leadership. *Super* leadership. *Principled* leadership. My favorites being *liquid* leadership, *food* leadership (seriously), and *boot strap* leadership. Go ahead, look for them on Amazon, or in the bookstore. They are there.

A good question to ask is, "Why are there so many books out there on leadership?" Other than because it is a popular topic and people want to make money by window dressing their own version of leadership, I can think of only one other connected reason: People want to understand leadership. They want to see how it's defined and how to "do" it. So, they buy the books.

We need leaders. We need them now more than ever. We long to be led. Really led. I don't care as much about the number of followers that a leader has as much as I want to see people using their lives to pursue something that they are passionate about and choosing to make the world a better place in a small (or large) way.

All of this brings me to this book. I am passionate about helping young people connect with the idea that they can lead. Not because they have a title next to their names, but because they have a passion, skill, or talent that the world needs, and they just haven't realized it yet. That is where the concept of emerging leaders comes into play. We need to do more to help leaders emerge, help young people, in particular, figure out that they can lead and know that we need them to lead. They don't have to be in front of the room, but they need to participate in the room. They don't need the title, but they need to act like they have it. They don't need followers, but they need to do something that is worth following. They need the patience to plant seeds, try new ideas, and fail miserably. Emerging leaders need our support, our encouragement, and our willingness to set them loose and figure it out on their own. We cannot weigh them down with the ideas of the past and how past generations saw leadership. They need to make their own meaning of the concept and wrestle in the mud with hard conversations that produce hard solutions. They need us to get out of their way and give them room to grow with their own understanding and vision. They need a guide, not a prescription.

Maureen has done an excellent job of providing the questions, but not the answers. She has cut through the complexity of the topic and framed the process of becoming a leader in a way that is simple, but not easy. The activities and conversations in this workbook will help readers figure out where they can best make a difference and, more importantly, what they need to do to make a difference.

Jim Collins said that the enemy of great is being good, and that is precisely why we have so few things and institutions that are truly great. We need to push, we need to engage, and we need to help others realize that they, too, have the *capability* to lead.

And then we can only hope that they *choose* to lead.

Enjoy the journey.

Paul Pyrz
President, LeaderShape

INTRODUCTION
INNOVATIVE LEADERSHIP

Leadership and innovation are two of the most compelling topics in business today. Yet despite the volume of resources exploring both topics, most approaches provide directional solutions that are merely anecdotal and lack sufficient information to actually allow leaders to make measurable change. We know that leadership plays a critical role in an organization's long-term success, and that innovation has become a strategic necessity in today's business environment. In short, both leadership and innovation have a greater impact today than ever before. Technology and increased access to information continue to accentuate their roles, yet organizations are often too overrun with change to handle the torrent of emerging demands.

Still, ensuing questions on how to lead and where to innovate remain puzzlingly philosophical: What is the role of leadership in a time of looming uncertainty? How will organizations innovate to overcome challenges that are largely unprecedented? In a new climate of business, what is the formula for creating success in both areas?

This workbook is designed to help answer those questions and help you to perform the critical self-evaluation needed to refine and innovate your own leadership skills. It is fundamentally about leadership, yet equally an account of applying innovation. Leadership needs innovation the way innovation demands leadership, and, by marrying the two, you can improve your capacity for growth and improved effectiveness.

This workbook explores a number of approaches to elaborate on both areas, not just conceptually, but tangibly, by providing exercises designed to enhance your leadership skills. Most importantly, any meaningful advancement concerning both must originate from you. In other words, becoming a better leader and optimizing innovation jointly hinge on your ability to authentically examine your own inner makeup, which will allow you to make real change.

At the same time, you must diligently address some challenging limitations. Despite their collective value, many conventional applications of leadership and innovation have often proven elusive and even problematic in real-world scenarios. For example, if the leadership team of a struggling organization drives initiatives that focus solely on making innovative changes to incentives, products, and services, without also advancing strategic purpose, culture, and team cohesiveness, they will ultimately miss the greater potential to create a meaningful turn-around in the organization. Productivity and system improvements are undoubtedly critical, but how employees make sense of their work experience is equally vital to team engagement and commitment. Innovating products and improving functionality—without also creating a better team environment or a more supportive organizational culture—often appears to pay off in the short term, yet produces lopsided decision-making and shortsighted leadership that have lasting adverse consequences.

Knowing that the future of organizations is irrevocably tied to a world of erratic change, we can no longer afford to improve our systems and offerings without equally advancing our leadership capacity. Leadership empathy and the ability to inspire cultural alignment, along with other important leadership activities, will make a significant impact on your organization and must be implemented as shrewdly as strategic planning.

Combining leadership with innovation, then, requires you to transform the way you perceive yourself, others, and your business. By vigorously looking into your own experience, including motivations, inclinations, interpersonal skills, and proficiencies, you can optimize your effectiveness in the current dynamic environment. Through deep examination and reflection, you learn to balance the hard skills you have acquired with meaningful introspection, all the while setting the stage for further growth. In essence, you discover how to strategically and tactically innovate leadership the same way you innovate in other aspects of your business.

Marrying Innovation and Leadership

Let's explore innovating leadership in a more tangible way by defining it in practical terms. This, of course, begs the obvious question: *what does innovating leadership really mean?*

It is important to first understand each topic beyond its more conventional meaning. For example, most definitions of leadership alone are almost exclusively fashioned around emulating certain kinds of behaviors: leader X did "this" to achieve success, and leader Y did "that" to enhance organizational performance.

Even if initially useful, such approaches are still, essentially, formulas for *imitating leadership*, and are therefore likely ineffectual over the long term. Innovating leadership cannot be applied as a monolithic theory, or as simple prescriptive guidance. It must take place through your own intelligence and stem from your own unique sensibilities.

In order to enhance this unique awareness process you will need a greater foundational basis from which to explore both topics, which means talking about them in a different context entirely.

Let's start by straightforwardly defining leadership:

> **Leadership is a process of influencing people strategically and tactically, affecting change in intentions, actions, culture, and systems.**

Within this context, and above all else, leadership involves a ***process of influence***: *strategic* influence to inspire vision and direction; *tactical* influence to guide functional execution.

Leadership influences individual intentions and cultural norms by inspiring purpose and alignment. It equally influences an individual's actions and organizational efficiencies through tactical decisions.

Innovation, as an extension of leadership, refers to the novel ways in which we advance that influence personally, behaviorally, culturally, and systematically throughout the organization.

> **Innovation is a novel advancement that influences organizations: personally, behaviorally, culturally, and systematically.**

Notice here that in addition to linking the relationship of leadership to innovation, we're also relating to them as an essential part of our individual experience. Just as with leadership and innovation, the way you uniquely experience and influence the world is defined through a mutual interplay of personal, behavioral, cultural, and systematic events. These same core dimensions that ground leadership and innovation also provide a context and mirror for *your total experience* in any given moment or on any given occasion.

Optimally then, leadership is influencing through an explicit balancing of those core dimensions. Innovation naturally follows as a creative advancement of this basic alignment. In our experience, leadership and innovation are innately connected and share a deep commonality.

Therefore, marrying leadership with innovation allows you to ground and articulate both in a way that can create a context for dynamic personal development—and dynamic personal development is required to lead innovative transformative change.

> **Innovating leadership means leaders influence by *equally* engaging their personal intention and action with the organization's culture and systems.**

Though we are, in a sense, defining innovative leadership very broadly, we are also making a distinct point. We are saying that the core aspects that comprise your experience—whether intention, action, cultural, or systematic—are inextricably interconnected. If you affect one aspect, you affect them all.

Innovative leadership is based on the recognition that these four dimensions exist simultaneously in all experiences and already influence every interactive experience we have. So if, for example, you implement a strategy to realign an organization's value system over the next five years, you will also affect personal motivations (intentions), behavioral outcomes, and organizational culture. Influencing one aspect—in this case, functional systems—affects the other aspects, since all four dimensions mutually shape that given occasion. To deny the mutual interplay of any one of the four dimensions misses the full picture. You can only innovate leadership by addressing reality in a comprehensive fashion.

Leadership innovation happens naturally and can be accelerated through the use of a structured process involving your own self-exploration, allowing you to authentically enhance your leadership beyond tactical execution.

To summarize, leadership innovation is the process of improving leadership that allows already successful leaders to raise the bar on their performance and the performance of their organizations.

An innovative leader is defined as someone who consistently delivers results using:

- **Strategic leadership** that inspires individual intentions and *goals* and organizational *vision and culture*;
- **Tactical leadership** that influences an individual's *actions* and the organization's *systems and processes*; and,
- **Holistic leadership** that aligns all core dimensions: *individual intention and action, along with organizational culture and systems.*

The Opportunity of Innovative Leadership

The overwhelming focus of today's organizational changes is on system functionality. Though necessary, it is only *part* of your total picture. Being guided by more strategically inclusive decisions may be the difference between managing failure and creating tangible success. Your leadership must consider a more balanced definition of innovation that comprehensively aligns vision, teams, and systems, and integrates enhanced leadership perspective with system efficiency.

This balanced approach to leadership and innovation is transformative for both you and your organization, and can help you to respond more effectively to challenges within and outside the enterprise. Innovating your leadership gives you the means to successfully adapt in ways that allow optimal performance, even within an organizational climate fraught with continual change and complexity. Conceptually, it synthesizes models from developmental, communications, and systems theories, delivering better insight than singular approaches. Innovative leadership gives you the capacity to openly recognize and critically examine aspects of yourself, as well as your organization's culture and systems, in the midst of any circumstance.

Defining What an Innovative Leader Does

What are specific behaviors that differentiate an innovative leader from a traditional leader? In this time of rapid business, social, and ecological change, a successful innovative leader is one who can continually:

- Clarify and effectively articulate vision
- Link that vision to attainable strategic initiatives
- Develop himself and influence the development of other leaders
- Build effective teams by helping colleagues engage their own leadership strengths
- Cultivate alliances and partnerships
- Anticipate and aggressively respond to both challenges and opportunities
- Develop robust and resilient solutions
- Develop and test hypotheses like a scientist
- Measure, learn, and refine on an ongoing basis

To further illustrate some of the qualities of innovative leadership, we offer this comparison between traditional leadership and innovative leadership:

TRADITIONAL LEADERSHIP	INNOVATIVE LEADERSHIP
Leader is guided primarily by desire for personal success and peripherally by organizational success	Leader is humbly guided by a more altruistic vision of success based on both performance and the value of the organization's positive impact
Leadership decision style is "command and control;" leader has all the answers	Leader leverages team for answers as part of the decision-making process
Leader picks a direction in "black/white" manner; tends to dogmatically stay the course	Leader perceives and behaves like a scientist: continually experimenting, measuring, and testing for improvement and exploring new models and approaches
Leader focuses on being technically correct and in charge	Leader is continually learning and developing self and others
Leader manages people to perform by being autocratic and controlling	Leader motivates people to perform through strategic focus, mentoring and coaching, and interpersonal intelligence
Leader tends to the numbers and primarily utilizes quantitative measures that drive those numbers	Leader tends to financial performance, customer satisfaction, employee engagement, community impact, and cultural cohesion

Getting the Most from the Workbook

Before you get started, take a moment to think about why you purchased this workbook. Setting goals and understanding your intentions and expectations about the exercises will help you focus on identifying and driving your desired results.

In order to help clarify, consider the following questions:

- What are the five to seven events and choices that brought you to where you are professionally and personally?
- How did these events and choices contribute to choosing to buy and use this workbook?
- What stands out in the list you have made? Are there any surprises or patterns?
- What do you hope to gain from your investment in leadership development?
- What meaningful impact will it produce in your professional career and personal life?

In addition to your reflection on the above questions, here are some ideas we recommend to help you get the most out of this experience. It is our observation that people who adhere to the following agreements tend to have a deeper and more enriching overall experience. By participating in this fashion, you will generate a richer evaluation of yourself and most effectively take advantage of what this workbook has to offer.

Take a moment to reflect on the guidelines:

AGREEMENT	RELATED ACTION OR BEHAVIOR
1. Be fully present	Let go of thoughts about other activities while you read. Bring your full attention to the work
2. Take responsibility for your own success	Be 100% responsible for the outcome of your engagement with this material
3. Participate as fully as possible	Complete all the exercises to the best of your abilities. Apply the concepts and skills that work best for you, and modify those that do not
4. Practice good life management	Invest time at scheduled intervals to work on the materials when you are mentally and emotionally at your best
5. Lean into optimal discomfort; take risks without overwhelming yourself	Be candid, open, and direct. Allow yourself to be curious and vulnerable
6. Take the process seriously, and more importantly take yourself lightly. Make this a positive and rewarding experience	Allow yourself balance. Find the lesson and humor in both your successes and mistakes. Most importantly, have fun!

How to Use the Workbook

After this introduction to innovative leadership, each subsequent chapter builds on a series of exercises and reflection questions designed to guide you through the process of developing your own abilities as an innovative leader. We recommend that you use the following sequence to help efficiently process the material:

1. Read Intently

Read through the chapter completely, as we introduce and illustrate an integrated set of concepts for each element in building innovative leadership.

2. Contemplate

Using a set of carefully chosen applications and specifically designed exercises will help you to embody the work and bring the concepts to life. Through a process of dynamic examination and reflection, you will be encouraged to contemplate some significant, real-life implications of change. Many of the exercises can be done on your own; others are designed to be conducted with input from your colleagues.

3. Link Together Your Experience

As you sequentially build your understanding, you will begin noticing habits and conditioned patterns that present you with clear opportunities for growth. Though you may encounter personal resistance along the way, you will also discover new and exciting strengths. As you become more adept at using these ideas, you will find yourself increasingly capable of proactive engagement with the concepts, along with an ability to respond to situations requiring innovative leadership with greater capacity.

Once you have completed the process, you will have created a plan to grow as an innovative leader. Ultimately, implementing that plan will be up to you and your team.

Innovative Leadership Assessment

Leadership Behaviors

Situational Analysis

Resilience

Developmental Perspective

Leader Type

Following is a short self assessment to help you identify your own innovative leadership scores. It is organized by the five domains of innovative leadership and will give you a general sense of where to focus your efforts to improve your innovative leadership and managerial capacity. As you progress through the book, you will find information on the full assessments if you are interested in a more in-depth and thorough analysis of your current capacity.

We encourage you to take this assessment as a way to get a snapshot of where you excel and where you may want to focus your developmental activities and energies.

Score Yourself on Awareness of Leader Type and Self-Management

Leadership Behaviors
Situational Analysis
Resilience
Developmental Perspective
Leader Type

Think about your level of response to work situations over the past year and answer the following questions using this scale:

Never (1)   Rarely (2)   Sometimes (3)   Often (4)   Almost always (5)

1. I have taken a leadership type assessment such as the Enneagram, Myers-Briggs Type Indicator or DISC, and used this information about myself to increase my effectiveness.   4   1 2 3 4 **(5)**

2. I use the insight from this assessment to understand my type—specifically, I understand my gifts and limitations, and try to leverage my strengths and manage my limitations.   3   1 2 **(3)** 4 5

3. I have a reflection practice where I understand, actively monitor and work with my "fixations" (a fixation is a negative thought pattern).   3   1 2 **(3)** 4 5

4. I have a clear sense of who I am and what I want to contribute in the world.   4   1 2 3 **(4)** 5

5. I manage my emotional reactions to allow me to respond with socially appropriate behavior.   3   1 2 3 **(4)** 5

6. I am aware of what causes me stress and actively manage it.   3   1 2 3 **(4)** 5

7. I have positive coping strategies.   3   1 2 3 **(4)** 5

8. I actively seek ways to feel empowered even when the organization may not.   3   1 2 3 **(4)** 5

24

Total Score

- If your overall score in this category is 24 or less, it's time to pay attention to your leadership type and self management.

  26
- If your overall score in this category is 25–31, you are in the healthy range, but could still benefit from some focus on your leadership type and self-management.

- If your overall score is 32 or above, Congratulations! You are self-aware and using your leadership type to increase your effectiveness.

  26   34

Score Yourself on Developmental Perspective Aligned with Innovation

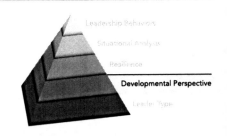

Think about your level of response to work situations over the past year and answer the following questions using this scale:

Never (1)   Rarely (2)   Sometimes (3)   Often (4)   Almost always (5)

1. I have a sense of life purpose and do work that is generally aligned with *4*   **1 2 3 (4) 5**
that purpose.

2. I am motivated by the impact I make on the world more than on personal notoriety. *5*   **1 2 3 (4) 5**

3. I try to live my life according to my personal values. *4*   **1 2 3 (4) 5**

4. I believe that collaboration across groups and organizations is important to *5*   **1 2 3 4 (5)**
accomplish our goals.

5. I believe that getting business results must be balanced with treating people *5*   **1 2 3 4 (5)**
fairly and kindly as well as have an impact on our customers and community.

6. I seek input from others consistently to test my thinking and expand my *4*   **1 2 3 (4) 5**
perspective.

7. I think about the impact of my work on the many elements of our community *3*   **1 2 (3) 4 5**
and beyond.

8. I am open and curious, always trying new things and learning from all of them. *4*   **1 2 3 (4) 5**

9. I appreciate the value of rules and am willing to question them in a *4*   **1 2 3 (4) 5**
professional manner.

Total Score

- ◢ If your overall score in this category is 27 or less, it's time to pay attention to your developmental level including testing your current level and focusing on developing in the area of developmental perspectives.

- ◢ If your overall score in this category is 28–35, you are in the healthy range, but could still benefit from some focus on developing in the area of developmental perspectives.

- *37* ◢ If your score is 36 or above, Congratulations! Your developmental level appears to be aligned with innovative leadership, yet this assessment is only a subset of a full assessment.

38

Score Yourself on Resilience

Think about your level of response to work situations over the past year and answer the following questions using this scale:

Never (1)   Rarely (2)   Sometimes (3)   Often (4)   Almost always (5)

1. I consistently take care of my physical needs such as getting enough sleep *2*   1 ②︎ 3 4 5
    and exercise.

2. I have a sense of purpose and get to do activities that contribute to that *2*   1 2 3 ④︎ 5
    purpose daily.

3. I have a high degree of self-awareness and manage my thoughts actively. *4*   1 2 3 ④︎ 5

4. I have a strong support system consisting of a healthy mix of friends, *2*   1 ②︎ 3 4 5
    colleagues, and family.

5. I can reframe challenges to find something of value in most situations. *4*   1 2 3 ④︎ 5

6. I build strong trusting relationships at work. *3*   1 2 3 ④︎ 5

7. I am aware of my own self-talk and actively manage it. *4*   1 2 3 ④︎ 5

8. I have a professional development plan that includes gaining skills and   1 2 ③︎ 4 5
    acquiring additional perspectives.
    4

Total Score   *24*

- ◗ If your overall score in this category is 24 or less, it's time to pay attention to your resilience.

- ◗ If your overall score in this category is 25–31, you are in the healthy range, but could still benefit *27* from some focus on resilience.

- ◗ If your score is 32 or above, Congratulations! You are likely performing well in the area of resilience, yet this assessment is only a subset of the full resilience assessment.

Score Yourself on Managing Alignment of Self and Organization

Think about your level of response to work situations over the past year and answer the following questions using this scale:

Never (1)   Rarely (2)   Sometimes (3)   Often (4)   Almost always (5)

1. I am aware of my own passions and values. 4   1 2 ③ 4 5

2. My behavior consistently reflects my goals and values. 3   1 2 ③ 4 5

3. I feel safe pushing back when I am asked to do things that are not aligned 3   1 2 ③ 4 5 with my values.

4. I am aware that my behavior and decisions as a leader have an impact on the 4   1 2 ③ 4 5 people I work with (even if I am not directly managing people).

5. I am deliberate about aligning my behaviors with the behaviors the 3   1 2 3 ④ 5 organization values and I pay attention to delivering the desired results (both results and behaviors).

6. I am aware of how my values align with those of the organization and where   1 2 ③ 4 5 they are misaligned; if there are misalignments, I try to find constructive ways address these differences. 3

Total Score

- ◤ If your overall score in this category is 18 or less, it's time to pay attention to your alignment with the organization and also the alignment of culture and systems within the organization that you are able to impact.

20   20◤ If your overall score in this category is 19–23, you are in the healthy range, but could still benefit from some focus on alignment.

- ◤ If your score is 24 or above, Congratulations! You are well-aligned with the organization and the organization's culture and systems are well-aligned.

Score Yourself on Leadership Behaviors

Leadership Behaviors
Situational Analysis
Resilience
Developmental Perspective
Leader Type

Think about your level of response to work situations over the past year and answer the following questions using this scale:

Never (1)   Rarely (2)   Sometimes (3)   Often (4)   Almost always (5)

1. I tend to be proactive – I anticipate what is coming next and actively manage 3   1 2 ③ 4 5
    it. (This may be primarily in my personal life.)

2. I focus on creating results in a way that helps me grow and develop along with   1 2 ③ 4 5
    those who work for me while accomplishing our tasks.   3

3. I think about the impact of my actions on the organization rather than just 4   1 2 3 ④ 5
    getting the job done.

4. I see how my work contributes to organizational success.   5   1 2 3 ④ 5

5. I deliberately try to improve myself and the organization.   4   1 2 3 ④ 5

6. I take time to mentor others, even when I am busy (this could be formal or 3   1 2 ③ 4 5
    informal mentoring).

7. I consider myself a personal learner because of the time I spend reading and 4   1 2 ③ 4 5
    trying new ideas and activities. I am curious.

8. I have the courage to speak out in a professional manner when asked to do 3   1 2 ③ 4 5
    something with which I disagree.

9. I accomplish results by working with and through others in a positive and 4   1 2 ③ 4 5
    constructive manner.

Total Score

- If your overall score in this category is 27 or less, it's time to pay attention to your leadership behaviors and look for ways to develop in alignment with your goals.

- If your overall score in this category is 28–35, you are in the healthy range, but could still benefit   30
  from some focus on your leadership behaviors.   32

- If your score is 36 or above, Congratulations! You are likely performing well in the area of leadership behaviors, but this assessment is only a subset of a full leadership behavior assessment.

CHAPTER 1
Elements of Innovative Leadership

In this chapter, we'll start with a discussion of innovative leadership that provides the general framework for innovating how you lead, then we'll go into what emerging leaders do in chapter two. Innovative leadership comprises the five elements presented and discussed below; these are then applied throughout the balance of the book.

Figure 1-1 Five Elements of Innovative Leadership

Leadership Behaviors

Situational Analysis

Resilience

Developmental Perspective

Leader Type

The five elements of innovative leadership are reflected in Figure 1-1.

What is truly unique in this approach to leadership is the overall comprehensiveness of the model. Theorists have looked at each of these elements separately for many years, and have suggested that mastering one or two of them is typically sufficient for effective leaders. We believe that while that may have been true in a less complex world, it is no longer the case. As the twenty-first century unfolds, the most effective leaders will need a much more holistic view than at any other time in history. In the following chapter, we will define and describe each individual element of innovative leadership and how they interact.

Leader Type

Part of the challenge in innovating leadership is learning to become more introspective and putting that introspective knowledge into practice. Looking inside yourself, examining the make-up of your inner being, enables you to function in a highly grounded way, rather than operating from the innate biases that lead to uninformed or unconscious decision-making.

First and foremost, when thinking about leadership, start by simply considering your disposition, tendencies, inclinations, and ways of thinking and acting. Innovating leadership hinges on understanding the simple manner in which you live in your life. One way to observe this is by examining aspects of your inner being, often called leader type, which reflect the leader's personality type. The Leader Personality Type (referred to going forward as Leader Type) has a critical influence on who you are as a leader. It is an essential foundation of your personal make-up and greatly shapes your leadership effectiveness. The ancient adage of "know thyself," attributed to various Greek philosophers, holds true as a crucial underpinning in leadership performance.

Your ability to use deep introspection relies on your development of a capacity for self-understanding and self-awareness. Both allow you to expand your perspective as well as build a greater understanding of others. These critical traits associated with leader type support a leader's abilities to manage self, communicate effectively with others, and encourage personal learning. You can use your understanding of your leader type (understanding yourself and others) as a powerful tool in effective leadership.

It is important to keep in mind that this particular notion of type is something that is native to your being and generally does not change significantly over the course of your life. This is an essential point: by understanding your type, as well as that of others around you, you can begin to see situations without the bias of your own perceptions. You have a clearer understanding, and can thus make more informed decisions with less speculation. You learn to deeply understand the inner movements of your strengths, weaknesses, and core patterns. Leadership typing tools are helpful in promoting this kind of self-knowledge and pattern recognition.

> *By learning about these patterns, you can gain perspective on your life and start connecting the dots among your different experiences. Most of us have a concept about how we behave, but that idea is likely clouded and not entirely true. One of the hardest things for most people is to see themselves accurately. How astonishing it is to see through the clouds and recognize yourself clearly.*
>
> — Roxanne Howe-Murphy, *Deep Living*

Learning at this deeper level from your own inner dynamics can offer remarkable insight into areas of your life that, in your own personal experience, you may either exaggerate or under emphasize.

Self-awareness and the capacity for self-management are foundational to innovative leadership and overall leadership effectiveness. By becoming aware of your inherent gifts as well as those of others, you are able to improve your personal effectiveness and that of the teams and departments with which you work.

Developmental Perspective

In this workbook we will be talking about *developmental levels and perspectives* as a core element in developing innovative leadership. Developmental perspectives significantly influence how you see your role and function in the workplace, how you interact with other people, and how you solve problems. The term *developmental perspective* can be described as "meaning making" or how you make meaning or sense of experiences. This is important because the algorithm you use to make sense of the world influences your thoughts and actions. Incorporating these perspectives as part of your inner exploration is critical to developing innovative leadership. In his best-selling business book *Good to Great*, author Jim Collins refers to Level 5 Leadership as an example of developmental perspectives applied to leadership. While we do not cover the relationship of Level 5 Leadership to developmental perspectives in this workbook, you can find more information on this subject in the *Innovative Leadership Fieldbook*.

Figure 1-2 Enneagram & Developmental Perspectives

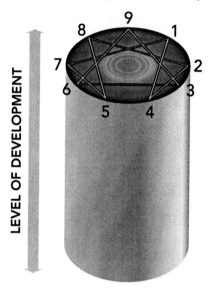

In order to connect developmental perspective with leader type, let's look at how these models come together. While leader type is generally constant over your life, you have the capacity to grow and develop your leadership perspective. In fact, leadership research strongly suggests that although your inherent leader type determines your tendency to lead, good leaders also develop over time. Therefore, it is often the case that leaders are perhaps both born and made. How leaders are made is best described using an approach that considers developmental perspective. Type remains consistent during your life while developmental perspective evolves. This is an important differentiator in leadership effectiveness and allows you to see what can be changed and what should be accepted as innate personality type.

We can also apply this model to the organizational level to help select and train leaders more effectively. Here are some additional benefits of using a model of developmental perspective:

- It guides leaders in determining their personal development goals and action plans using developmental perspectives as an important criteria.

- It is important to consider when determining which individuals and team members best fit specific roles.

- It helps in identifying high-potential leaders to groom for growth opportunities.

- It helps in the hiring process to determine individual fit for a specific job.

- It helps change agents understand the perspective of others and craft solutions that meet the needs of all stakeholders.

Figure 1-3 Maslow's Hierarchy of Needs

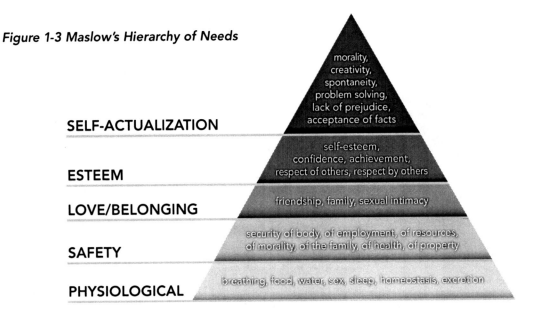

The developmental perspective approach is based on research and observation that, over time, people tend to grow and progress through a number of very distinct stages of awareness and ability. One of the most well-known and tested developmental models is Abraham Maslow's *hierarchy of needs*, a pyramid-shaped visual aid Maslow created to help explain his theory of psychological and physical human needs. As you ascend the steps of the pyramid you can eventually reach a level of self-actualization.

Developmental growth occurs much like other capabilities grow in your life. Building on your leader type, you continue to grow, increasing access to or capacity for additional skills. We call this "transcend and include" in that you transcend the prior level/perspective and still maintain the ability to function at that perspective. Let us use the example of learning how to run to illustrate the process of development. You must first learn to stand and walk before you can run. And yet, as you eventually master running, you still effortlessly retain the earlier, foundational skill that allowed you to stand and walk. In other words, you can develop your capacity to build beyond the basic skills you have now by moving through more progressive stages. It is also important to note that while individuals develop the ability to run, there are many times that walking is a much more appropriate choice of movement. The successful leader has a broad repertoire of behavior and is able to select the most appropriate one depending on the situation.

People develop through stages at vastly differing rates, often influenced by significant events or "disorienting dilemmas." Those events or dilemmas provide opportunities to begin experiencing your world from a completely different point-of-view. The nature of those influential events can vary greatly, ranging from positive social occasions like marriage, a new job or the birth of a child to negative experiences, such as job loss, an accident or death of a loved one. These situations may often trigger more lasting changes in your way of thinking and feeling altogether. New developmental perspectives can develop very gradually over time or, in some cases, emerge quite abruptly.

Some developmentally advanced people may be relatively young and yet others may experience very little developmental growth over the course of their life. Adding to the complexity of developmental growth is the fact that the unfolding of developmental perspectives is not predictably based on age, gender, nationality, or affluence. We can sense indicators that help us identify developmental perspective when we listen and exchange ideas with others, employ introspection, and display openness to learning. In fact, most people very naturally intuit and discern what motivates others as well as what causes some of their greatest challenges.

We believe a solid understanding of developmental perspectives is critical to innovating leadership and encourage you to delve into this concept in much greater detail. The purpose of this workbook is to introduce you to the concepts.

Resilience

There are two distinct ways to understand resilience. First, using an engineering analogy, resilience is viewed as how much disturbance your systems can absorb before a breakdown. This view highlights the sturdiness of individual systems. Second, from a leadership perspective, resilience can be viewed as the ability to adapt in the face of erratic change while continuing to be both fluid in approach and driven toward attaining strategic goals. The first definition reflects stability and the second refers to fluidity and endurance. Addressing all aspects of resilience is critical to optimizing it.

Among the elements essential to leadership, resilience is unique in that it integrates the physical and psychological aspects of leader type and developmental perspective to create the foundation of a leader's inner stability. This foundation enables you to demonstrate fluidity and endurance as you adapt to ongoing change.

Figure 1-4 Elements of Resilience

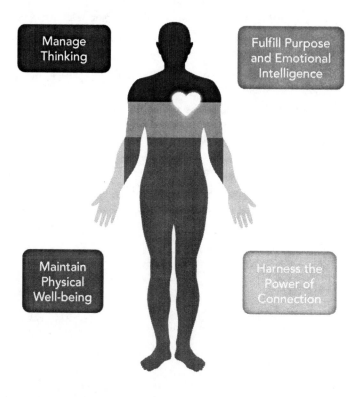

The underlying premise of resilience is that leaders need to be physically and emotionally healthy to do a good job. In addition to physical and emotional health, the resilient leader also has a clear sense of life purpose, strong emotional intelligence, an effective capacity to manage thinking, and strong supportive relationships. For most people, enhancing resilience requires a personal change.

Our model has four categories, shown in Figure 1-4. They are: maintain physical well-being, manage thinking, fulfill purpose using emotional intelligence, and harness the power of connection. These categories are interlinked, and all of them must be in balance to create long-term resilience.

Often, leaders we work with initially say they are too busy to take care of themselves. Finding the balance between self-care and meeting all of our daily commitments is tough. Most people fall short of their goals and over the longer term make choices for or against their resilience and personal health. Our message here is that creating and maintaining resilience is essential to your success. As you improve your resilience, you will think more clearly and have a greater positive impact in your interactions with others; investing in your resilience supports the entire organization's effectiveness.

The following table provides questions for each of the four resilience categories to identify opportunities for improvement.

TABLE 1-1 KEYS TO BUILDING & RETAINING PERSONAL RESILIENCE

Manage Thinking	Fulfill Life Purpose
Practice telling yourself: - Challenges are normal and healthy for any individual or organization - My current problem is a doorway to an innovative solution - I feel inspired about the opportunity to create new possibilities that did not exist before	Understand what you stand for. Maintain focus. Ask: - What is my purpose? - Why is it important to me? - What values do I hold that will enable me to accomplish my purpose? - What opportunities do I have in my professional life that help me achieve my life purpose?
Maintain Physical Well-being	**Harness the Power of Connection**
Are you getting enough: - Sleep - Exercise - Healthy Food - Time in nature - Time to meditate & relax Are you limiting or eliminating: - Caffeine - Nicotine	Practice effective communication: - Say things simply, and clearly - Make communication safe by being responsive - Encourage people to ask questions and clarify if they do not understand your message - Balance advocacy for your point with inquiring about the other persons' points - When you have a different point of view, seek to understand how and why the other person believes what they do in a non-threatening way - When in doubt, share information and emotions - Build trust by acting for the greater good

Situational Analysis

Though much of the work of building innovative leadership is based on an in-depth examination of your personal and professional experience, understanding the background or context of that experience is equally important. Consider that your experience isn't merely a collection of personal expressions, events, and random happenstance; rather, it is fundamentally shaped by the background interplay of your individual attributes, shared relationships, and involved organizations.

Every moment of experience is influenced by a mutual interaction of self, culture, action, and systems. All four of these basic dimensions are fundamental to every experience we have. Situational analysis involves evaluating the four-dimensional view of reality shown in Figure 1-5. This comprehensive approach ensures that all dimensions are aligned, resulting in balanced and efficient action. We refer to these four dimensions as self, action, culture, and systems. This balance—without favoring elements—is an important skill for innovative leaders.

Leaders often take a partial approach to changing organizations. They over-emphasize systems change with little or no consideration to the culture or how their personal views and actions shape the content and success of the change. This multi-dimensional approach provides a more complete and accurate view of events and situations. Situational analysis enables you to create alignment across the four dimensions on an ongoing basis.

Figure 1-5- Integral Model

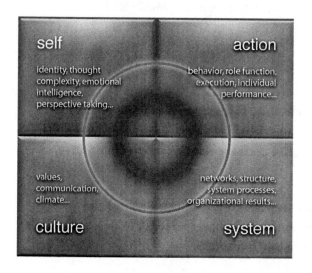

American-born philosopher Ken Wilber developed a conceptual scheme to illustrate the four basic dimensions of being that form the backbone of experience. His Integral Model provides a map that shows the mutual relationship and interconnection among four dimensions where each represents basic elements of human experience.

When you use situational analysis, you are cultivating simultaneous awareness of all four dimensions. Let's look at an example. This is a sample narrative taken from Integral Life Practice (Wilber et al) that will give you a more experiential description of how these dimensions shape every situation in your life.

Example: *"Visualize yourself walking into an office building in the morning..."*

Self *(Upper-Left Quadrant, "I"):* You feel excited and a little nervous about the big meeting today. Thoughts race through your head about how best to prepare.

Culture *(Lower-Left Quadrant, "We"):* You enter a familiar office culture of shared meaning, values, and expectations that are communicated, explicitly and implicitly, every day.

Action *(Upper-Right, "It")*: Your physical behaviors are obvious: walking, waving good morning, opening a door, sitting down at your desk, turning on the computer, and so on. Brain activity, heart rate, and perspiration all increase as the important meeting draws nearer.

System *(Lower-Right, "Its")*: Elevators, powered by electricity generated miles away, lift you to your floor. You easily navigate the familiar office environment, arrive at your desk, and log on to the organization's intranet to check the latest sales numbers within the organization's several international markets.

In applying situational analysis to an organizational change, you would be aware of the four dimensions as referenced above and, when changing one, you would consider the impact on the others. If you get promoted and want to be perceived differently, how will you behave in the situation above? What will be different in all four dimensions as you walk into the office building?

A crucial part of innovating leadership is developing your capacity to be aware of all dimensions of reality in any given moment and identify misalignments. Even though you cannot physically see the values, beliefs, and emotions that strongly influence the way an individual colleague perceives himself and the world, nor a group's culture, emotional climate or collective perception, they still profoundly shape the vision and potential of leaders to innovate.

Situational Analysis is an innovative leadership tool that allows you not only to make more informed decisions, but also helps you optimize performance within yourself, your teams, and the broader organization. The alignment of all dimensions is the key to optimizing performance.

Leader Behaviors

Let's now shift our focus to the actionable craft of leadership. This section is as about observable leadership capability comprising hard skills and their associated behaviors. Leadership hard skills and behavior are critical to success, and serve as objective performance measures of innovative leadership.

Hard skills, knowledge, and aptitude fall into two primary categories: industry-related and functional. Leadership skills can be evaluated by observable behaviors and result from specific kinds of knowledge, skills, and aptitudes that are centered around leadership.

Thus, we use the term leadership behaviors in this workbook any time when referring to observable, actionable leadership traits. Both hard skills and leadership behaviors are critical to building innovative leadership. The balance between the importance of hard skills and leadership behaviors will shift as the leader progresses in the organization with leadership skills and behaviors becoming increasingly important with career advancement.

Leadership behaviors are important because they are the objective actions the leader takes that impact organizational success. We have all seen brilliant leaders behave in a manner that damages their organization and we have seen other leaders continually behave in ways that promote ongoing organizational success. Effective leadership behaviors drive organizational success and, conversely, ineffective leadership behaviors drive organizational dysfunction or failure. Even the most functionally brilliant leader must demonstrate effective leadership behaviors to be successful when leading an organization.

To be successful, a leader must possess the hard skills in organizational administration to understand how the organization operates and the leadership behaviors to be able to effectively lead. If either of these sets of skills is missing, the leader and the organization are at risk of failure. Early in a leader's career, mastery of organizational leadership set him apart from his peers. As he progressed into senior leadership ranks and ultimately to the role of executive, his use of leadership behaviors became his primary focus while he never lost the need for hard skills; now, he relies on his functional and leadership skills to guide his direction and action.

There are different ways to discuss leadership from a skills perspective as demonstrated by Peter Northouse in his book on leadership.

> *There are several strengths in conceptualizing leadership from a skills [actions] perspective. First, it is a leader-centered model that stresses the importance of the leader's abilities, and it places learning skills at the center of effective leadership performance. Second, the skills approach describes leadership in such a way that it makes it available to everyone. Skills are behaviors that we all can learn to develop and improve. Third, the skills approach provides a sophisticated map that explains how effective leadership performance can be achieved.*
>
> **— Peter G. Northouse, *Leadership Theory and Practice***

As a leader, it is important to understand the key leadership behaviors important to you and your organization. With this understanding, you can determine where you excel and where you may want to refine your skills.

The Leadership Circle Profile (LCP) Behaviors

Figure 1-6- The Leadership Circle Profile

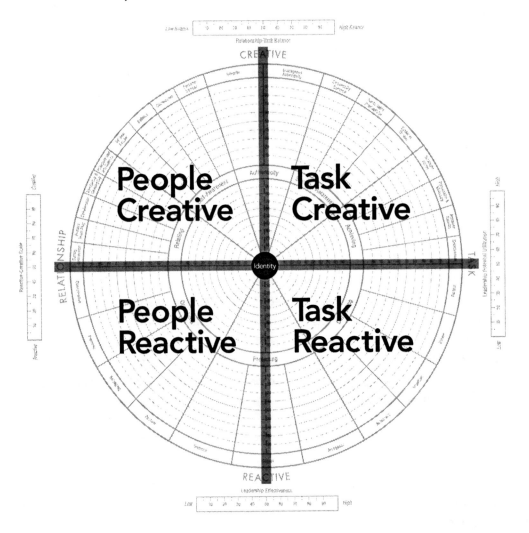

The Leadership Circle measures key dimensions of leadership shown in the inner circle in Figure 1-6. The sub-categories are shown in the outer circle (for reference go to www.theleadershipcircle.com) and can be broken into four key dimensions: people creative, task creative, people reactive, and task reactive. These four categories are created by drawing a line through the circle horizontally to separate the creative and reactive dimensions. The second line is drawn vertically to separate the people and task dimensions. The top of the circle behaviors are *creative behaviors*:

- ◢ Relating
- ◢ Self-awareness
- ◢ Authenticity
- ◢ Systems Awareness
- ◢ Achieving

These behaviors reflect proactive action which is referred to by the Leadership Circle as "Creative." These behaviors reflect behaviors associated with setting strategic direction and inspiring people to accomplish goals.

The behaviors in the bottom half of the circle are *reactive behaviors*. They reflect <u>inner beliefs that limit effectiveness, authentic expression, and empowering leadership</u>. These dimensions reflect behaviors associated with following direction or reacting to circumstances as they arise rather than setting direction and creating the conditions for success.

The creative and reactive dimensions are then split on the vertical axis between people and task behaviors. People behaviors are associated with the actions leaders take to build themselves and their people such as relating and self-awareness. The task behaviors are actions leaders take associated with the work of running a business, such as systems awareness and achieving. The degree of emphasis on task versus relating will vary depending on your level within the organization, the overall organizational structure, and the organizational type. What is important to note is that leadership requires a balance of task-related behaviors along with relationship-related behaviors and this balance changes depending on the situation.

It is important to understand the behaviors associated with innovative leadership and also be able to flex your own leadership behaviors to match what is required by the organization. The most effective leaders and organizations demonstrate behaviors heavily weighted on the creative end of the scale. The balance between task and relationship will depend in part on the role of the leader within the organization. Strong leaders have the capacity to perform both people- and task-related roles well.

According to *The Leadership Circle Participant Profile Manual*, 2009 Edition published by The Leadership Circle, "These competencies [behaviors] have been well researched and [are] shown to be the most critical behaviors and skill sets for leaders." Table 1-2 was adapted from *The Leadership Circle Participant Profile Manual*, 2009 Edition, published by The Leadership Circle.

TABLE 1-2 LCP DIMENSION DEFINITIONS

Creative leadership behaviors listed below reflect key behaviors and internal assumptions that lead to <u>high fulfillment, high achievement leadership</u>.

The **Relating** Dimension measures leader capability to relate to others in a way that brings out the best in people, groups and organizations. It is composed of:	The **Self-Awareness** Dimension measures the leader's orientation to ongoing professional and personal development, as well as the degree to which inner self-awareness is expressed through high integrity leadership. It is composed of:
<ul><li>Caring Connection</li><li>Fosters Team Play</li><li>Collaborator</li><li>Mentoring and Developing</li><li>Interpersonal Intelligence</li></ul>	<ul><li>Selfless Leader</li><li>Balance</li><li>Composure</li><li>Personal Learner</li></ul>

TABLE 1-2 LCP DIMENSION DEFINITIONS (CONT.)

The **Authenticity** Dimension measures the leader's capability to relate to others in an authentic, courageous, and high integrity manner. It is composed of: • Integrity • Authenticity	The **Systems Awareness** Dimension measures the degree to which the leader's awareness is focused on whole system improvement and on community welfare (the symbiotic relationship between the long-term welfare of the community and the interests of the organization). It is composed of: • Community Concern • Sustainable Productivity • Systems Thinker
The **Achieving** Dimension measures the extent to which the leader offers visionary, authentic, and high accomplishment leadership. It is composed of: • Strategic Focus • Purposeful and Visionary • Achieves Results • Decisiveness	

We will use these creative behaviors throughout the book as we refer to leadership behavior.

The next chapter will discuss emerging leadership in additional detail and talk about specific areas that are critical to success at the emerging leadership level.

Developing Innovative Leadership

Chapters three through seven walk you through the process of developing innovative leadership specifically for managers and emerging leaders. Each chapter reflects one step in the development process and includes tools, templates, questions for reflection, and an example of a person who has completed the process. It is the comprehensiveness of this reflection coupled with the exercises that will give you insight into yourself and your organization. This insight is required to change yourself and your organization concurrently or to manage your internal change in the context of an organization that you cannot or do not want to change. It is important to note that leadership development is an ongoing process. Upon completion of this process you will be more effective; yet, depending on your objectives, you may still want to continue developing. Figure 1-7 below shows the six steps in the process of innovative leadership development.

Figure 1-7 Leadership Development Process

While this process appears linear, we have found that when leaders work through these steps they often return to earlier parts of the process to clarify and sometimes change details they had originally thought were correct. The structure of our process will continue to challenge you to refine the work you have accomplished in prior tasks. First ideas are often good ones, but when you work with this tool you will continually find insight and discover new things. We encourage you to continue to test your ideas and feel comfortable going back in the process for further refinement.

The time you spend on the workbook is an investment in your development. If you are engaging deeply in the process it will likely take you three to six months or longer to complete. Whether managing personal and organizational change, or internal change alone in the context of an organization that you cannot or do not want to change, reflection and thorough evaluation are required. This reflection will take time and is critical to your growth. We strongly encourage you to engage in the process with as much time and attention as possible. The value you ultimately take from this process is closely linked to the time you invest.

REFLECTION QUESTIONS

What innovative challenges does your organization face?

How does your organization support effective leadership for innovation?

In which ways would you consider yourself an innovative leader?

How do you personally connect with leadership and innovation?

Where are the opportunities for you to be an innovative leader?

What would make you and your organization more effective in leading innovation beyond products, services, and systems?

CHAPTER 2
Fulfilling the Role of an Emerging Leader

The scope of this workbook is on the leadership level of manager and emerging leader. We first share our definition of what an emerging leader is in the context of innovative leadership; then, we apply our interactive six-step Leadership Development Process to this stage. We include tools and practices for each step in the process designed to support and enhance practical effectiveness for an emerging leader at this particular stage of the innovative leadership journey. The steps in this process are:

Each step of the process poses reflection questions geared toward an emerging leader. When coupled with hands-on exercises, it is our hope that the reader gains insight that is specifically targeted to the emerging leader level of the innovative leadership journey.

In the introduction, we asserted that leadership innovation is a *process of improving leadership* that allows already successful leaders to raise the bar on personal and organizational performance. By adopting this view of leadership as an improvement process, we can assume that there are various stages of maturity an individual will demonstrate at any given point in the journey to become an innovative leader as reflected in Table 1-1. As an emerging leader, you may not see yourself as an already successful leader, but as a new leader. If this is where you see yourself, you will be building new skills and also building on the skills you developed in leading yourself.

Our series of workbooks is designed to help individuals at each organizational level toward innovative leadership. This table walks you through some of the criteria we evaluate when determining the leadership stage. Work focus is the level of responsibility you take on during a normal work week; decision time horizon refers to the general timeframe considered when you make decisions; and complexity is the level of your tasks—this could include the intricacy of a single task, or are managing many tasks, projects, processes, and even systems or enterprises.

TABLE 2-1: THE INNOVATIVE LEADERSHIP DEVELOPMENT CONTINUUM

Stage	Work Focus	Decision Time Horizon	Complexity
Lead Self	Mainly task	1 day – 2 years	Few tasks/projects focus on task level
Emerging Leader	Mainly task and management – small leadership (focus on process)	3 months – 5 years	Begin focus on process – small to medium-sized project and small to medium-sized team. Set vision for department within organization, or vision for small organization. Begin to show concern about impact on the larger stakeholder group and community
Leader	Balance lead and management – some task (focus on process and system)	3 – 10 years	Manage multiple complex projects, manage medium to large team. Set vision for division or small to medium-sized company. Growing concern with the larger community and industry (beyond company)
Executive	Mainly lead – for some still heavy management – little task (focus on system and systems within larger systems)	5 – 20 years	Manage/lead complex enterprise – often global (company, nonprofit, or public service). Integrated focus – set vision, drive culture, and systems. Also interact and influence larger system—such as industry and government—that interact with the enterprise

By using *the Innovative Leadership Development Continuum,* an individual can create a development plan that is more relevant to his personal journey.

What is an Emerging Leader?

In the context of the Innovative Leadership Development Continuum, the emerging leader represents the second of four stages. At this level, you shift from primarily leading self to leading and managing others. While still focused on completing assigned tasks that are routine in nature, you increasingly assign and manage the work of others and/or are responsible for the completion of sequential activities (a process). As the scope, complexity, and time horizon of a position increases, you typically need to evolve their developmental perspective in order to be effective.

While every organization has its own unique structure, we can use a few universal categories to describe what an emerging leader is and what an emerging leader typically does in a variety of contexts. However, regardless of the context, by using these categories, we want the reader to gain a clear sense of what we mean by "emerging leader."

The following section describes the job requirements of an emerging leader through the lens of what you might typically see on a performance evaluation. Using the six-step leadership process will help you improve how you perform against these criteria, as well as help you clarify your vision and values to ensure you are working in an organization where you will perform at your best.

Work Focus

While an individual's work in the "Lead Self" stage is typically focused on executing individual tasks that are assigned and monitored by someone else, the "Emerging Leader" stage demands that the individual take more responsibility for leading and/or influencing others. You will be expected to understand broader team goals that are set by a superior, then identify and prioritize daily activities for yourself and/or your team to meet these agreed goals. This shift in focus toward a broader team-based perspective means that you may increasingly coordinate, supervise, and manage the work of other team members. If you do not have a formally-assigned supervisory role, at a minimum you will be expected to provide guidance to and develop less experienced personnel.

As you begin to master the new territory of leading others and handling more complex work assignments, your level of influence in the organization will, typically, continue to rise. You may be required to provide recommendations on policy and/or process improvements, as well as provide input regarding the development of new procedures for your area of responsibility. If you have a supervisory role, you will start to plan and prioritize more complex activities for the team.

In most cases, at the "Emerging Leader" stage, the individual will need to operate more independently, receiving less and less guidance or instruction over time. This marks another fundamental shift from the "Lead Self" stage in which you are typically dependent upon someone else to assign tasks and to solve problems. Along with the ability to influence others, your level of independence can be viewed as a primary key indicator of how much you are emerging as a leader in the organization.

It is important to point out that this stage is additive. Typically, an increase in responsibility does not replace the obligation to complete some tasks; rather, the individual will be expected to increase his capacity in a way that he can perform both effectively. Therefore, it is critical that the individual progressing to this stage find ways to build and unleash his leadership capabilities. The following section describes five specific developmental areas that are critical for emerging leaders to focus on when building skills.

Scope and Complexity

While in the "Lead Self" stage the individual may be primarily responsible for simply completing distinct tasks in one or a few well-defined work streams. While moving toward the "Emerging Leader" stage, you may become accountable for the results of a project or a broad scope operation with a moderate level of ambiguity, risk, unpredictability, and diversity. In real terms, this usually translates into the individual being responsible for the output of multiple work streams that have a larger impact on the organization than during the "Lead Self" stage. With this increase in scope, you will not have the ability to "do it all yourself," and will need to depend on others more and more to accomplish tasks. This required interdependence with others is a key shift from the "Lead Self" stage.

The work performed by an individual at the "Emerging Leader" stage typically increases to a moderately complex level. While in the "Lead Self" stage you typically perform well-defined tasks that have a clear beginning, end, and outcome, in the "Emerging Leader" stage you will need to complete tasks that may have several possible resolutions. This will require you to build and apply a more sophisticated level of problem-solving, sharpening your ability to understand interdependencies, evaluate multiple potential outcomes, and propose possible solutions. In addition, the emerging leader will be increasingly asked to complete more advanced tasks that build upon the foundation of knowledge and skills established in the "Lead Self" stage.

Decision Impact

There are two characteristics of decisions that fundamentally change in the "Emerging Leader" stage: (1) the routine level; and (2) the required use of stronger judgment. This change requires you to adopt a more sophisticated level of decision-making. Further, you will find that his decisions will increasingly have a bigger impact on others. The "Emerging Leader" stage typically brings more complex problems to solve and advanced tasks to complete.

The discrete and well-defined nature of tasks in the "Lead Self" stage typically means that the work is more repetitive and predictable than in later leadership levels, and you make decisions that are more routine in nature that require less judgment. Generally, a boss is available to address difficult challenges and guide the individual contributor. In other words, the decisions required are more "black and white" with a greater likelihood that there are simply two ways to take action: right or wrong. Additionally, the consequence of your decisions typically only impacts your own work, with little potential to affect others on the same team.

Financial Control

In the "Leading Self" stage, you typically receive defined task assignments to complete, with little to no focus on associated budgets. The "Emerging Leader" stage marks the first time you may be expected to have a level of financial responsibility as a part of your job requirement.

At a minimum, you may be expected to understand how your actions impact costs, and then how to use this information as input into assigning and completing work tasks. The overall goal is to give you more responsibility for organizational financial performance by requiring you to adhere to capital and operating budgets provided.

As you continue to mature in the "Emerging Leader" stage, you may begin to participate in the processes of budgeting and reporting, and may start to manage small budgets yourself by coordinating your team's work within guidelines.

Financial acumen, while an important skill to master for anyone working in an organizational context, becomes more critical as you continue to progress as a leader and is an important component of any leadership development plan.

Knowledge and Expertise Level

To be effective and to meet the increased demands of the "Emerging Leader" stage, you will need to demonstrate a higher level of competence in his professional or technical field and are expected to build and apply an intermediate to comprehensive knowledge of your professional or technical field. You will be expected to learn standard or conceptual methods or principles and adapt them as needed to real-life situations.

To lead or influence, you will need to establish personal credibility with others, which partly means proving to them that you have a requisite level of knowledge or expertise in the topic at hand. In addition, your effectiveness in handling increased scope and complexity will also rest on your ability to build knowledge and expertise.

Over time, you will be considered a senior knowledge resource for your professional or technical field. As such, you will be expected to provide guidance and/or instruction to less-experienced personnel.

People Management and Development

Central and critical to all of the changing demands associated with the "Emerging Leader" stage is the increased importance of effectively leading and managing others. In this capacity, you will be expected to take on more responsibility for both managing and developing others.

The management of others may take the form of a supervisory role (formal or informal), where you will begin to assign, coordinate, and monitor tasks being completed by other team members. You will increasingly be held accountable by superiors for successful outputs from the team. In essence, your success will become much more dependent upon ensuring the success of others. This is a key shift from the "Leading Self" stage in which you are typically only responsible for the completion of your own work.

Regardless of whether you take on a supervisory role or not, you will be expected to develop the knowledge, skills, and abilities of others. This new responsibility is typically a function of your higher level of experience and proficiency. In the "Lead Self" stage, you will typically build a foundation of knowledge and skills associated with your professional or technical field that becomes important to share and transfer to others. Your ability to impart this learning is a key factor in ensuring the long-term health and viability of any team or organization.

Ultimately, to be successful as an emerging leader, you will need to inspire trust to bring out the best in others. Inspiring trust is certainly a complex process in itself, but one of the most important success factors is the ability to relate and connect with others. This is only achieved by individuals who commit to an ongoing professional and personal development of interpersonal intelligence and self-awareness. The more you align your own thoughts, feelings, and beliefs with the actions and behaviors you exhibit, the more likely you will be successful in building trust—and, therefore, effective in leading others.

Summary

An individual operating at the "Emerging Leader" stage typically will be characterized by the following:

- A **work focus** that is a blend of managing and/or influencing others while completing assigned tasks that are advanced in nature.
- Work that is of moderate **scope and complexity**.
- **Making decisions** that are non-routine, that require judgment, and primarily have an impact on your own team, and possibly other teams.
- A basic understanding of **financial impact** of actions and decisions, with limited **budget control**.
- An intermediate to **comprehensive knowledge** of the professional or technical field.

Using this as a working definition for an emerging leader, we'll now turn our attention toward how you might use the six-step Innovative Leadership Development Process to improve your effectiveness at this specific stage.

CHAPTER 3
Step 1: Create a Compelling Vision of Your Future

The Innovative Leadership workbook is designed to provide a step-by-step process to support you in developing your own innovative leadership capacity. The fieldbook that serves as the foundation for this workbook has been tested with a broad range of clients, as well as with hundreds of working adults participating in an MBA program.

The comprehensiveness of these exercises coupled with reflection exercises will give you the insight into yourself and your organization needed to make substantive personal change. While this process appears linear, we have found that when leaders work through these steps, they often return to earlier parts of the process to clarify and sometimes refine their answers. The structure of our process will continue to challenge you to refine the work you have completed in prior exercises. First ideas are often good ones, yet when you work with this tool you will continually find insight. We encourage you to continue to test your ideas and feel comfortable circling back for further refinement.

These tools differ from many others by directing you through an exploration that takes into account your unique, individual experience while simultaneously considering the groups and organizations to which you belong.

The first step in starting your development process is cultivating a sense of clarity about your overall vision, which can also be summarized as your direction and aspirations. The intention behind your aspirations fuels both personal and professional goals, as well as provides a sense of meaning in your life. When your actions are aligned with your goals, they drive the impact you create in the world at large. As you move forward in the visioning process, we will guide you to begin thinking about individuals or groups who inspire or have a significant influence on you.

Simply put, your vision and aspirations help you decide where best to invest your time and energy, and clarifying them helps you define a manner of contributing to the world that authentically honors who you are. Your vision and aspirations further help you clarify what you want to accomplish over time. You can select the time span that resonates for you, whether short-term—one to five years— or perhaps a longer-term time horizon, such as the span of your lifetime. After clarifying your own unique, personal vision, you will have the foundation for your ensuing change process. Knowing your vision and values creates the basis for your goals, and can help you align your behavior with your aspirations.

As part of the visioning process, it is important to consider the context of your leadership role, your organization, and your employer. If you are clear about your personal vision, you can evaluate where and how you fit within that organization. On the other hand, if your vision differs significantly from what you do and how you work, the additional information will guide you in finding a role that is a better fit (this transition may not happen in the short term). By knowing your vision and aspirations, you are equipped with information that helps you align the energy you invest with the work you do.

In addition to creating a well-defined vision, it is also important to be clear about your motivation. The combination of vision and desire is what will enable you to maximize your potential. Without sufficient desire, solid vision, and understanding of your current capabilities, you are likely to struggle when progress becomes difficult.

Tools and Exercises

The exercises will guide you in identifying what is most important to you. First, you will define your future, and from that vantage point, clarify your vision and values. You will then consider what you want to do professionally, as well as the type and extent of the impact you want to have on the world.

It is important to note that many people will complete this exercise and still not have a clearly articulated vision—this is because defining personal vision requires a great deal of introspection for most people. While some people grow up knowing what they want to do for a living, others find that identifying a vision is a process of gradual exploration and will take more time and energy than completing a single workbook exercise. You will likely refine your vision as you progress through later chapters in the workbook, based on the information you learn about yourself. Because the visioning process is iterative in nature—a process of self-discovery—the exercises in this book will serve as the foundation for a longer process that may take considerably more time to complete. It will likely change as you gain experience and as your introspective process matures.

Define Personal Vision

Follow the steps defined below:

Step 1: Create a picture of your future. Imagine yourself at the end of your life. You are looking back and imagining what you have done and the results you have created.

- What is the thing of which you are most proud?
- If you had a family, what would they say about you?
- What did you accomplish professionally?
- What would your friends say about you?

For the rest of this exercise, let that future person speak to you and help you set a path that will enable you to look back with pride and say things like, "I feel fulfilled and at peace. I lived my life well."

Step 2: Write a story. Now that you have that image of what you will accomplish, write a brief story about your successful life. Include details about the questions above. Make it a story of what you went through to accomplish each of the results for the questions you answered. What you are trying to create is a roadmap for your journey that gives you more insight into what you would want if you had the option to design your perfect life.

- Who helped you along the way?
- What did you enjoy about your daily life?
- Who was closest to you?
- What feelings did you have as you accomplished each milestone along the way?
- How did you mentor others and contribute to the success of others?
- What did you do to maintain your health?
- What role did spirituality or religion play in your journey?
- What job did you have?
- What role did material success play in your life?
- What type of person were you (kind, caring, driven, gracious)?

Step 3: Describe your personal vision. Given the story you have written and the qualities you demonstrated, write a two to five sentence life-purpose statement—a statement that talks about your highest priorities in life and your aspirations. This statement should capture the essence of how you want to live your life and project yourself.

> *An example - My vision is to develop myself to my greatest capacity and help others develop and thrive in all aspects of their lives. I will live consciously and courageously, relate to others with love and compassion, and leave this world better for my contribution.*

Step 4: Expand and clarify your vision. If you are like most people, the choices you wrote are a mixture of selfless and self-centered elements. People sometimes ask, "Is it all right to want to be covered in jewels, or to own a luxury car?" Part of the purpose of this exercise is to suspend your judgment about what is "worth" desiring, and to ask instead which aspect of these visions is closest to your deepest desire. To find out, ask yourself the following questions about each element before going on to the next one: If I could have it now, would I take it?

Some elements of your vision don't make it past this question. Others pass the test conditionally: "Yes, I want it, but only if..." Others pass, but are later clarified and distilled in the process. As you complete this exercise, refine your vision to reflect any changes you want to make.

After defining and clarifying your vision, it is time to consider your personal values. The combination of these two exercises will help you create the foundation of what you want to accomplish and the core principles that guide your actions as you work toward your vision.

Checklist for Personal Values

Values are deeply held views of what we find worthwhile. They come from many sources: parents, religion, schools, peers, people we admire, and culture. Many go back to childhood; others are taken on as adults. Values help us define how we live our lives and accomplish our purpose.

Step 1: Define what you value most. From the list of values (both work and personal), select the ten that are most important to you as guides for how to behave, or as components of a valued way of life. Feel free to add any values of your own to this list.

PERSONAL VALUES CHECKLIST

- Achievement
- Advancement and promotion
- Adventure
- Arts
- Autonomy
- Challenge
- Change and variety
- Community
- Compassion
- Competence
- Competition
- Cooperation
- Creativity
- Decisiveness
- Democracy
- Economic security
- Environmental stewardship
- Effectiveness
- Efficiency
- Ethical living
- Excellence
- Expertise
- Fame

- Intellectual status
- Leadership
- Location
- Love
- Loyalty
- Meaningful work
- Money
- Nature
- Openness and honesty
- Order (tranquility/stability)
- Peace
- Personal development/learning
- Pleasure
- Power and authority
- Privacy
- Public service
- Recognition
- Relationships
- Religion
- Reputation
- Security
- Self-respect
- Serenity

PERSONAL VALUES CHECKLIST (CONT.)

- Fast living
- Fast-paced work
- Financial gain
- Freedom
- Friendships
- Having a family
- Health
- Helping other people
- Honesty
- Independence
- Influencing others
- Inner harmony
- Integrity

- Sophistication
- Spirituality
- Stability
- Status
- Time away from work
- Trust
- Truth
- Volunteering
- Wealth
- Wisdom
- Work quality
- Work under pressure
- Other: _____

Step 2: Elimination. Now that you have identified ten values, imagine that you are only permitted to have five. Which five would you give up? Cross them off. Now cross off another two to bring your list down to three.

Step 3: Integration. Take a look at the top three values on your list.

- How would your life be different if those values were prominent and practiced?

- What does each value mean? What are you expecting from yourself, even in difficult times?

- Does the personal vision you've outlined reflect those values? If not, should your personal vision be expanded? Again, if not, are you prepared and willing to reconsider those values?

- Are you willing to create a life in which those values are paramount, and help an organization put those values into action?

Which one item on the list do you care most about?

Putting Vision into Action

After defining and clarifying your vision and values, the next step is to reflect on how to put them into action. You will consider the things you care about most as well as your innate talents and skills to determine what about your current life you would like to refine, or even change. You are probably passionate about specific interests or areas within your life; if you're really fortunate, you will have opportunities to participate in one or more of those areas.

The purpose of this exercise is to consider how best to incorporate your passions into how you make a living. You likely have passions that will always remain in the realm of hobbies; the main point of the exercise is to move closer to identifying your passions and expressing them in as many areas of life as possible.

In our experience, part of figuring out what you want to do is paying attention to what you find profoundly interesting. Those interests simply reveal themselves in the course of your daily interaction with peers and colleagues, and quite frequently at business functions. They are reflected in whatever you find yourself reading; they even display themselves in the context of more casual occasions, and are often seen in activities shared among friends.

This is the type of exercise that appears very simple on the surface, and may be something you revisit annually in order to refresh what is genuinely important to you. We find that revisiting allows you to nurture a sense of continual clarity about your direction. Iteration provides a mechanism for clarifying your direction as you grow and develop. With everything you try (false starts and all) you will discover a deeper truth about yourself that moves you closer to your most authentic passions. Some of those passions will be incorporated into your career; other passions help shape your personal life.

Exercise: Putting Vision into Action

Step 1: Identify your foundation. Answer the three questions below by compiling a list of responses to each.

- What are you passionate about? This will come from the prior exercise and should now be relatively concise.

- What meets your economic needs?

- What can you be great at?

Note - Your answers to these questions should reflect your values from the Personal Values Checklist.

Step 2: Review and identify overlap. Review your answers and identify the overlaps.

Step 3: Harvest the ideas. Based on the overlaps, do you see anything that might be incorporated in what you do or how you work? This could mean adding an additional service line to an existing business or allocating a portion of your work time to a project that is aligned with your values.

An example of this is a client who, based on significant reflection, learned he valued giving back to the community in a way that he was not doing at the time. He was the CEO of a technology firm. His passion was offering computer training for returning veterans; he maintained the job of CEO and added a community support function into his business. His passion for service to the community and his professional skills afforded him the ability to follow his passion and still run a successful business. In the process of following his passion, he is building the workforce in his community and building his reputation as a civic leader and successful entrepreneur.

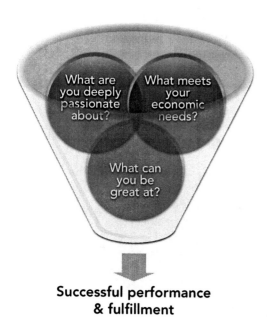

**Successful performance
& fulfillment**

Vision-Based Actions

Innovative Leadership Reflection Questions

To help you develop your action plan, it is time to further clarify your direction using the reflection questions below. "What do I think/believe?" reflects your intentions. "What do I do?" questions reflect your actions. "What do we believe?" reflects the culture of your organization (i.e., work, school, community), and "How do we do this?" questions reflect systems and processes for your organization. This exercise is an opportunity to practice innovative leadership by considering your vision for yourself and how it will play out in the context of your life. You will define your intentions, actions, culture, and systems in a systematic manner.

Table 3-1 contains an exhaustive list of questions to appeal to a broad range of readers. You will likely find that a few of these questions best fit your own personal situation. Focus on the questions that seem the most relevant to you. We recommend you answer one to three questions from each category.

TABLE 3-1: QUESTIONS TO GUIDE THE LEADER AND ORGANIZATION

What do I think/believe?

- How do I see myself in the future? What trends do I see around me that impact this view? Have I considered how these trends impact the way I want to contribute?
- How does my view of myself impact me? Am I inspired by my vision? Terrified?
- How do I see myself within the larger environment? This can range from my family, the organization, to the global environment.
- After doing the exercises, what is my vision?
- After doing the exercises, what are my values? What do I stand for? What do I stand against?
- What are the connections between my business vision and my personal mission, passion, and economic goals?

What do I do?

- How do I gather input from key stakeholders to incorporate into my vision (family, business, self)?
- How do I research trends that will impact my industry so I can understand my future placement and how to navigate potential transitions in my industry?
- How do I synthesize competing goals and commitments to create a vision that works for me in the context of the communities I serve (family, friends, work, and community)?
- How do I develop my vision taking the greater economic conditions into account?
- What do I tell others about my vision? Do I have an "elevator speech"? Is it something I think is inspirational?

What do we believe?

- How does my personal vision fit within the larger context of my family, my community, my industry or my job?
- How do I create a shared belief that my vision will help the organization succeed within the larger community and also help the community succeed?
- What do we believe we stand for as an organization? How should we behave to accomplish what we stand for (guiding principles/values)? Do my values align with the organizational values?
- How do I reconcile differences between my values and those of my organization? How will these differences impact my ability to develop toward my vision and goals?

How do we do this?

- How do I monitor the organization's impact on my vision? How do I honor my vision when helping define/refine the organizational vision?
- What is our process for defining/refining changes to our shared vision for the organization and other systems I function within? What is our process for clarifying and documenting our values? How do I ensure that my values are aligned with our guiding principles?
- Who gives me feedback on their perspective of my progress? How often? What form would I like this feedback to take?
- What measures help me determine progress toward my vision and values? How do I track and report progress toward these goals? Is my behavior supporting the organizational goals? Are the organizational goals supporting my goals?

Because there are many different ways to interact with the workbook, we have two case studies. Our emerging leaders have either answered different questions, or approached the exercises in slightly different ways to demonstrate the range of options for working with the exercises. We recommend you find the approach that best meets your needs and fits your style.

To help illustrate these reflection questions, we've included Jonathan's and Demetrius's answers. We have tried to capture their internal thought process in these exercises in a way that is rare in a business context, but helpful for the purpose of personal development.

Introduction to Jonathan

Jonathan graduated from the University of Urbana in 2011. He is a graduate of the LeaderShape program where he initially clarified his personal vision. He is founder and president of Illini Prosthetic Technologies (IPT) technologies which he started in 2008.

IPT's focus is to re-enable amputees around the world with simple, innovative, and affordable solutions. He now provides technical and business leadership to operations in Latin America, and interfaces IPT with hospitals, clinics, and NGOs working with amputees in Latin America.

Its goal is to disseminate its unique technology, and comparable technologies, to disadvantaged individuals around the world through partnerships with clinics and aid organizations active in all parts of the world to: provide solutions to disadvantaged individuals who previously have not had access to affordable care; increase the effectiveness of aid organizations operating in the developing world; and, create social value within the framework of a financially sustainable nonprofit.

Jonathan's Personal Vision Defined

Step 1: Create a picture of your future. Imagine yourself at the end of your life. You are looking back and imagining what you have done and the results you have created.

- **What is the thing of which you are most proud?** I am most proud of raising a family which is united and shares similar values to mine, while having spent my career improving the lives of others. I am at peace because I know where I have been, where I am, and where I am headed, and I know that my life was a genuine one.

- **If you had a family, what would they say about you?** They always completely felt my love for them, they loved being loved by me and loving me, and I taught them the core values that enabled them to live out their dreams. They will miss me a great deal after I am gone, but will use this emotion to become great people in their own lives.

- **What did you accomplish professionally?** I brought hope and results to a lot of people who lived with almost nothing, and who then went on to do the same thing for others. This was made possible through my founding of and leading a number of socially-minded organizations and movements.

- **What would your friends say about you?** They loved being with me, remember a lot of great experiences together, and were inspired by my life. They will also miss me a great deal when I am gone, but, like my family members, they will go out and do great things.

Step 2: Write a story.

- **Who helped you along the way?** I was helped by my faith, my family, my friends, my mentors, and my colleagues. I surrounded myself with people I knew would help me to make visions come true.

- **What did you enjoy about your daily life?** I most enjoyed being around the people I love and the people I care about, while constantly fighting for the people I wanted to help. I also enjoyed being able to work independently of the rigorous structure and societal expectations that come with a bureaucratic organization, and being able to diversify my efforts among many things which interested me. Every day was a new adventure which challenged me to be the best I could be and taught me new things.

- **Who was closest to you?** My wife, children, brothers, and parents were closest to me. My mentors and friends were also very close to me.

- **What feelings did you have as you accomplished each milestone along the way?** I felt incredibly excited about the human impact we (my team and I) had made, and was ready to start on my next project of making an impact in the lives of others. It was refreshing to switch into a new project every so often—this is what kept me sharp my entire career.

- **How did you mentor others and contribute to the success of others?** I mentored those who were in project teams with me to grow into leadership roles as I moved on to form new teams. Their success as future leaders in the organizations which I founded was equally important as was the metricized success of the organizations which they were leading. These leaders who I coached from peer co-founders to the future leaders of my organizations went on to form more organizations and perpetuate the founding-coaching-transition model. The ripples in the pond grew to affect a lot of people in very good ways.

- **What did you do to maintain your health?** I ate healthily, exercised regularly, and abstained from the things which I knew would degrade my health without good return. My relationships kept me accountable to this healthy way of life, and provided me with everything I needed emotionally. My continued education kept my mind developing throughout my career. My commitment to my faith kept my spirit renewed and refreshed every day of my life.

- **What role did spirituality or religion play in your journey?** My faith is the most important foundation in my life because it explains why I am in this world, how I should live and for what purpose, and where I am headed after I die. I attended religious services each week and maintained a daily routine of prayer and devotion in order to maintain spiritual health.

- **What job did you have?** I had the job of applying my social and technical passions to helping those in need around the world. This was manifested through my founding and leadership of a number of socially-minded organizations (both for-profit and nonprofit) which collectively worked on a number of pressing social issues (healthcare, education, poverty, etc.).

- ➤ **What role did material success play in your life?** Material items played an extremely small role in my happiness. The only major things I spent major money on were: my children's education, my home, and traveling the world. Much of my money was invested into other socially-minded organizations that were doing work in which I believed.

- ➤ **What type of person were you (kind, caring, driven, gracious)?** I was a person who had his priorities straight and stayed true to his values. When I worked, I was an inspirational, innovative, and driven person who had an excellent rapport with others, but when I was not working I was a fun-loving, light-hearted family man.

Step 3: Describe your personal vision.

My vision was to spend my life making a positive impact on those who live in constant need, empowering them to do the same for others. I did this while building other visionaries who made their impact on the world, the most important of whom are the members of my family.

Step 4: Expand and clarify your vision.

My vision is to spend my life positively impacting those who live in constant need, empowering them to do the same for others. I will do this in a way that my family and I can emotionally and financially sustain, and, in the process, build my children and colleagues into great leaders who are also focused on human impact.

Jonathan's Checklist for Personal Values

Step 1: Define what you value most.

Relationship with my Creator; love for and from my family; honesty and trust in all parts of life; hope in people; longevity in relationships; physical and mental health; challenging, stimulating, and diversified work; family and work balance; learning and excellence in work; worldly view and experience.

Step 2: Elimination. Now that you have identified ten values, imagine that you are only permitted to have five. Which five would you give up? Cross them off. Now cross off another two to bring your list down to three.

(1) Spiritual relationship; (2) love for and from my family; (3) honesty and trust.

Step 3: Integration. Take a look at the top three values on your list.

- ➤ **How would your life be different if those values were prominent and practiced?** I would commit more time to my faith and to my family, even at the expense of the progress that I have every day in my work. I already practice honesty and trust in all aspects of my life.

- **What does each value mean? What do you expect from yourself, even in difficult times?** (1) My relationship with my Creator means an intimate spiritual connection, and my resulting way of life. I should be taking more time for daily prayer and devotion, and doing a better job of aligning my actions and strategy against the parameters of my faith. Though I am increasingly busy with my work, this should only increase the devotion I have to this value in my life. (2) My love for and from my family means that I am continually renewing and growing my relationships within my family (including my brothers, parents, grandparents, and significant other). I should be spending more time to connect with each person in my family, and to give them love and receive their love. Again, this should only increase in magnitude as time goes on. (3) My honesty and trust in all parts of life means that I am maintaining full integrity in all that I do professionally and personally. I feel like this is the value in which I am doing the best I can right now because, for me, this must be foremost in all things. I will never compromise this value and, thus, it remains at a high level of importance regardless how busy I am.

- **Does the personal vision you've outlined reflect those values? If not, should your personal vision be expanded? Again, if not, are you prepared and willing to reconsider those values?** My personal vision is built upon these values. My desire to serve others through my vision directly stems from my spiritual beliefs. This value also gives rise to my extremely high value on family and on integrity. My vision specifically discusses my desire to help others (and to help them help others), and it mentions that I want to train my family members to do the same. I should probably retool my vision statement to be more inclusive of my value of honesty and to include family more comprehensively than just training my family members to carry out a similar type of work. Because my values set my compass, I should reword my vision statement and not the values which have created it.

- **Are you willing to create a life in which these values are paramount, and help an organization put those values into action?** Without hesitation, yes.

Which one item on the list do you care most about?
If I need to list only one, my spiritual relationship is the value of highest importance to me.

Jonathan's Putting Vision into Action Exercise

Step 1: Identify your foundation. Answer the three questions below by compiling a list of responses to each.

- **What are you passionate about?** I am passionate about global problems and solutions (especially in regards to health), socially-minded organizations, employing science and engineering to solve problems, teaching others to make an impact, writing and speaking in public, my family life, my faith life, working and visiting new parts of the world.

- **What meets your economic needs?** I can make a solid living from becoming an expert on global health problems and solutions.

■ **What can you be great at?** I can be really great at leading socially-minded organizations and efforts which are working to solve global health issues.

Step 2: Review and identify overlap. My answers to "what I can be great at," "what meets my economic needs," and "what am I passionate about" all line up very nicely with my revised vision statement. They all also implicitly involve the top three values I chose, as well as the original ten that I started with.

Step 3: Harvest the ideas. For me, this analysis is really a reaffirmation of the work I am currently doing with the nonprofit organization that I founded and for which I now work fulltime. This does give me solid direction for my personal future following my current mission with this organization, as I begin to apply to graduate schools in the field of public health and think about where I am headed in the five- to ten-year timeframe in my global health work. Looking at this is very important for me because it helps me to know what experiences I need to get prior to starting graduate school so that I can use that education to position myself in the niche of the global health community about which I am most passionate.

What do I think/believe?

■ *How do I see myself in the future? What trends do I see around me that impact this view? Have I considered how these trends impact the way I want to contribute?*

In the future, I see myself as a constant social innovator. I have started and led a number of successful organizations focused on a set of global problems, and I already have an idea for the next organization which I will form to address a specific need. I continually see the new face of a problem which has not yet been solved, and I see new technological and business development that could be applied to that problem to solve it. I also see increased societal support for socially-focused innovation which continually feeds resources to these organizations.

What do I do?

■ *How do I gather input from key stakeholders to incorporate into my vision (family, business, self)?*

I constantly surround myself with people who have knowledge and experience in the areas in which I am working, and use their input to reach decisions that I make within my organization and my life. I consider each person a mentor, and establish that fact from the first time that we meet so that they know how much their wisdom means to me and they are committed to the success of that which we discuss. It is important to get input from multiple sources and to remember that at times it will be conflicting. At the end of the day, the important thing is that I choose which input to follow, and that I never feel pressured to implement input that does not feel consistent with my vision.

What do we believe?

- *How does my personal vision fit within the larger context of my family, my community, my industry or my job?*

  My life vision is currently manifested in the mission of my nonprofit organization, which is to produce and distribute prosthetic arms to amputees living in poverty. While this is the present manifestation of my vision, I know that it is only the current step in my lifelong journey to fulfill my vision. My family, friends, and community are very much supportive of how I am currently pursuing my vision, and so are the amputees and organizations that will benefit from using our prosthetic arm.

- *How do I create a shared belief that my vision will help the organization succeed within the larger community and also help the community succeed?*

  I founded my organization based upon my original vision, and worked hard to inspire my business partners to take part in this vision and to share it with others. Each of my partners had different personal motivations to share in this vision, but each of us is united in a common end-goal. The organizations our nonprofit are partnered with also share in the common end-goal, as do their patients. While all parties approach goals in different ways, we all agree what the goal is and, thus, work together in the effort. This is shared belief in our vision on both team and community levels.

- *What do we believe we stand for as an organization? How should we behave to accomplish what we stand for (guiding principles/values)? Do my values align with the organizational values?*

  We advocate for amputees who need our product, and the comprehensive process of developing, testing, manufacturing, and distributing the product which gets us there. Every organization providing the device to a patient is our top priority. A sub-value of that larger value is producing a quality product and providing a quality service. My personal values very much align with these organizational values because they focus on helping people.

- *How do I reconcile differences between my values and those of my organization? How will these differences impact my ability to develop toward my vision and goals?*

  While my personal values or style can sometimes be slightly different than those of the organization, they are very similar; and, I would not have much interest working in an organization in which this was not the case. This alignment is present because I am the founder of the organization, and have instilled a lot of the current culture and values. This is a key advantage to founding one's own organization instead of assimilating into one, and it is the reason that founding an organization is often times the most efficient and accurate way to implement a personal vision. Although we work in the context of social service, it is very important that we look after our personal needs for enrichment and growth—this is sometimes hard to do with such a small staff that is so determined to accomplish a singular mission.

How do we do this?

■ *Who gives me feedback on their perspective of my progress? How often? What form would I like this feedback to take?*

As mentioned above, I have a group of mentors with whom I meet on a regular basis to discuss professional and personal matters. They have all come to know me well enough that they can help me to evaluate tough decisions that I face in terms of my vision. My personal preference is to meet with at least one of my personal mentors once a week in person.

Introduction to Demetrius

At age 33, Demetrius, a successful senior project manager and former computer engineer, began an MBA program to expand his understanding of how businesses function and to grow his leadership skills. On a daily basis, he is involved in face-to-face communications with various stakeholders in addition to leading his teams through the ambiguity of project definitions to successfully deliver high-quality products to the sponsor and the organization.

Demetrius's Vision Development Process Vision of the Future

When I look into the future I want to be proud of the person I have become and the life that I have lived. In particular, I want to ensure that my wife and I have raised a beautiful family in which our children think independently and are able to articulate their own personal visions. I would like for my children to be able to say I have been there for them every step of the way, and allowing them to experience life while guiding them away from danger when possible. For me, family and family interactions are highly valued, so the closest people to me are my wife and our children. However, I don't discount the close friends I have known since high school and those I've met along the journey since college.

Professionally, I want to create an organization whose culture represents my personality: relaxed and laid back, yet focused and driven. I want to create a work environment in which people are excited about their work and where they can accomplish their professional goals. Finally, my organization must take into account our community and find ways to give back every chance we get.

Demetrius's Vision

My vision is to develop myself to my greatest capacity and create a healthy and loving environment in which my family will thrive. I strive to be a friend who can be counted on in every way. I will create a business that delivers value to our clients and community, and has a culture where people can thrive and grow personally.

Demetrius's Values

Top three values:

1. Family

2. Integrity

3. Humility

What do I think/believe?

- *How do I see myself in the future?* One thing I have always believed to be a constant in my life is that change is inevitable. As a leader, I believe it is my responsibility to my organization and to the teams that I lead to embrace and prepare for change. I see myself being the conduit to change that will enable growth for me, my family, and my peers, company, and community. I believe individuals are more willing to accept change if they have a roadmap to guide them. If I understand the potential risks and rewards associated with any forthcoming change, I can plan a course of action that will enable me to capitalize on the rewards, while mitigating or eliminating the risks. I also understand that I will not have an answer for everything, and when a situation arises I still need to stay levelheaded and forward-thinking to help guide the aforementioned groups through the process of change.

- *How does my view of myself impact me? Am I inspired by my vision? Terrified?* After completing my undergraduate degree in computer science engineering, I began reading a variety of books that I didn't pick up while in school. One such book was *Think and Grow Rich* by Napoleon Hill. In his book I found a common theme that has become the basis for many aspects of my life: A made up mind is the most powerful thing a person can have. So, am I inspired by my vision? Absolutely! I envisioned myself walking across the stage as a graduate, I envisioned contributing at a high level within my organization, I envisioned leading—and not simply managing—teams. In each vision I could see the impact it would have on me and the people around me. With each vision, I made up my mind that it was the right thing for me to do and I let that vision guide me to reach my goals.

  At the same time, I am mindful that there is still a ton of growth and learning that I have to do in my career and in my personal life. I make it a point to learn from everyone around me and in each encounter that I have. Every individual has some knowledge that they can share—intentionally or not—if you take the time to listen.

- *How do I see myself within the larger environment? This can range from my family, the company, to the global environment?* As the father of a seven-month-old daughter, the way I see myself has completely changed because I am now the center of her world. Having a child puts a lot of environmental concerns into focus that I didn't necessary think too much about before she was born. I have always been a big believer in volunteerism and lending a hand, but I never thought much about what the world would look like when my child was older. I now make more deliberate and conscious efforts to be a positive influence in my physical environment and have increased my volunteer activities.

What do I do?

- *How do I gather input from key stakeholders to incorporate into my vision (family, business, self)?*
I recently had a conversation with my wife about my vision for my career. In particular, do I continue to work toward becoming a 'C' level executive within an organization, or do I turn my attention to owning my own business. I have also spoken with colleagues and previous supervisors about their assessment of my strengths and weaknesses. I have asked these groups of individuals because I trust they will provide honest feedback—whether they may or may not agree with my own assessment of myself. While I'm not looking for them to make a decision for me, I do value their opinions and their viewpoints. At the end of the day, I will take time to internalize the information that I have received from them to formulate a plan of action, but the final decision will be made after some introspection.

- *How do I synthesize competing goals and commitments to create a vision that works for me in the context of the communities I serve (family, friends, work, and community)?*
For me this has been a constant dilemma. While I believe in putting my family above all else, I also know there are times that I have to put work first to create a better sense of stability for my family. The way I handle this is to envision the future I want for my family and set incremental milestones to achieve those goals. One such goal was going back to school and completing my MBA. This meant sacrifices on my wife's part, but at the same time we knew that if I completed the program quickly it would have less of an impact on our family and a bigger reward in our future.

As part of setting those milestones, my wife and I periodically revisit them to see what is still relevant and make course corrections to ensure we are still on path, or, if need be, forge a new path.

What do we believe?

- *How does my personal vision fit within the larger context—my family, my community, my industry, my job?*

When I look at my industry, I begin to feel more and more confident that my personal vision is aligned with the visions of my industry. We have begun the transformation from managing people to leading people. The time has passed from command and control, to lead and learn. There is more power in thinking and working as a group, as opposed to any one person feeling as if he needs to have all the answers. This is the vision I have working for an organization and leading an organization into the future.

My wife and I also share a vision as we move forward with our careers and our lives. The sharing of the vision is an important concept. Of course we are two different individuals with different goals, but the vision we share is in the support that we show each other. It's really important to each of us that we are each other's biggest supporter. Therefore, we make it a point to help each other to grow and to help each other to achieve individual personal goals.

- *What do we believe we stand for as an organization?*

As an organization we stand for providing the best in value to our customer while maintaining integrity in the work that we produce. For me, there is a lot to be said about doing the "right thing." As an organization, of course, we are concerned about the bottom line, but not at the expense of doing something that our customers would deem unethical or not in their best interests. This is a type of organization that I can stand behind and I believe that we are headed in the right direction. At this point, I believe my values are becoming more closely aligned with our organizational values and this is a positive sign.

How do we do this?

- *Who gives me feedback on their perspective of my progress? How often? What form would I like this feedback to take?*

I believe feedback comes in many forms and it comes on a daily basis. For example, when we conduct product reviews with our clients, I take a scan of the individuals to gain a general sense of the feeling within the room. Then, as the presentation comes to a close, I begin to listen to feedback. If I notice a look of concern or confusion, I make it a point to ask the individual about any concerns. This gives people an opportunity to voice any issues they have, and it gives me an opportunity to clear up any confusing points. The feedback given at these reviews is directed at the team, but it's also an indirect indication of the job that I'm doing.

I also use a more direct approach of simply asking for feedback on a regular basis. I'm a firm believer of not waiting until a yearly review to give feedback to members of my team, or to find out how I'm progressing. If you wait until the end of the year or you wait until your yearly review, it's too late to change something that happened six months earlier. However, if I am actively seeking feedback on a regular basis, I can make course adjustments and I have a better chance to correct the behavior before my annual review.

- *What measures help me determine progress toward my vision and values? How do I track and report progress against these goals? Is my behavior supporting the organizational goals? Are the organizational goals supporting my goals?*

As a practicing project manager, I believe in periodically checking progress on my primary projects. The same is to be said about my vision, my values, and my goals. When it comes to my values, I'm constantly making sure that I'm staying true to them and take time to ensure that my values are still in line with my visions of the future. At the same time, I use my short- and long-term goals as stepping stones to the next portion of my vision of the future. I work to keep my values, short- and long-term goals aligned so that as I complete one set of goals and approach the next, I can start working on generating the next set of goals that are necessary to actualize my vision.

Your Process of Creating a Compelling Vision

Now that you have read Jonathan's and Demetrius's personal narratives, it is time to complete the exercises and answer the questions for yourself. We encourage you to complete all of the exercises. These exercises establish a strong foundation for your personal vision, values, and course of action, so exercise patience and give yourself time to explore your hopes and dreams as authentically as possible. You will know you've completed this step and are ready to move to the next when you feel you have created a vision and set of values that truly inspire you.

Throughout this chapter, we have discussed exercises that will help you clarify your life direction and create a compelling vision for your own life and work. The next chapter focuses on assessing where you are right now in your career and personal development.

What do I think/believe?

What do I do?

What do we believe?

How do we do this?

CHAPTER 4
Step 2: Analyze Your Situation and Strengths

Now that you have developed (or refined) your vision, it is time to examine your strengths and development opportunities. This step will help you refine and clarify those strengths and weaknesses using standard assessment tools. You will then decide which areas you would like to improve by building on what you already do well and addressing weaknesses. We recommend using a general guideline that focuses 80% of your effort on building your existing strengths and 20% on addressing weaker areas. Though this a general approximation, the 80/20 rule is a directional one stemming from the belief that you are already successful and have simply taken the opportunity to further advance and refine your capabilities. If you find serious deficiencies, those deficiencies can be best addressed by other leadership books and resources.

It is important to combine your vision with a firm understanding of your current performance, abilities, and personality type. The data will help you become more aware of your strengths and weaknesses, and also clarify how others see you. The combination of information will help you determine the gap between your current state (based on assessment data) and your vision.

It's important to note that many people have a higher capacity than they are able to use at work. This could be caused by working in a job that does not use your full abilities. When you begin taking assessments, it will be important to get information from a broad range of sources to ensure you have a clear and accurate picture of your true capacity.

Assessment Tools

One of the primary ways to help you understand your current development and performance is using a combination of assessments to measure your current skills and abilities, along with your personality style and developmental perspective. This should allow you to identify the gap between your present state and what you need to fulfill your vision.

There are several good assessments available. The tools we suggest have been used extensively with our clients and are recommended with a high degree of confidence. We find that each provides vital information in helping to convey a comprehensive picture of strengths, weaknesses, and opportunities. These assessments are aligned with the five elements of innovative leadership discussed in chapter one. Some are expensive and require a skilled coach to interpret them; this

Leadership Behaviors

Situational Analysis

Resilience

Developmental Perspective

Leader Type

option is not practical for everyone. Metcalf & Associates has created a free online assessment that does not replace the detailed assessments recommended below, but does offer a high-level view of your innovative leadership and can indicate key areas of focus. It can be accessed by going to http://www.metcalf-associates.com/innovative-leadership-assessment.html.

The tools we use to help develop innovative leaders are:

- **Leader Type Assessment using the Enneagram**

We recommend using the Enneagram first and foremost to <u>discover your own personality type</u> and, as appropriate, to determine the types of those with whom you interact. The Enneagram is used for personal growth, relationships, therapy, and in the business world as an indicator of an individual's primary personality type. The <u>*Riso-Hudson Enneagram Type Indicator*</u> (version 2.5) provides a reliable, <u>independently scientifically validated</u> tool for that purpose. Finding your type is not the final goal, but merely the starting place for working with our system, and embarking on a fascinating and rewarding journey of self-reflection.

The Enneagram helps you to see your *own* personality dynamics more clearly. Once you are aware of the importance of personality types, you see that your own style is not equally effective with everyone. One of the Enneagram's most useful lessons is how to move from a style of interacting in which others are expected to mold themselves to your way of thinking and values to a more flexible style in which you act from an awareness of the strengths and potential contributions of others. By doing so, you help others become more effective themselves—and as a result, harmony, productivity, and satisfaction are likely to increase. The Enneagram is an inexpensive assessment that is available online and does not require a certified coach to interpret (source: www.enneagraminstitute.com/practical.asp).

- **Developmental Perspective**

We recommend the Maturity Assessment Profile (MAP) to evaluate developmental perspective. Dr. Susanne Cook-Greuter developed this assessment to describe developmental perspectives as part of her Ph.D. at Harvard University. It is widely considered one of the most rigorously validated, reliable, and advanced assessment tools used to evaluate adult leadership development. Participants taking the assessment complete thirty-six sentence stems about various topics. The freeform response format allows test takers to provide a wide range of information, which gives the scorer ample data to evaluate varying developmental features along three main lines: cognitive complexity, emotional affect, and behavioral. The combination of the three allows the scorer to determine the action logic, that is, how people tend to reason and respond to life. It is critical for you to be completely open and honest when taking this assessment in order for there to be sufficient data to provide an accurate score. The MAP assessment is available through Pacific Integral (www.pacificintegral.com) or Susanne Cook-Greuter (www.cook-greuter.com). This assessment requires a coach to interpret the data and comes with a detailed report explaining the developmental levels and the perspectives each offers.

Resilience Assessment

Metcalf & Associates created a basic tool to help you assess your attitudes and practices that help support resilience, and identify areas where you can further build your capacity. It is based on fundamental stress management research including the characteristics that support "stress hardiness," a concept pioneered by Suzanne Kobasa. This assessment can be found at http://www.metcalf-associates.com/resilience-assessment-tool.html.

Competency Assessment

It is important for a leader to have an accurate view of what others see to be able to make appropriate changes and gauge the impact of these changes. There are many ways to develop a deeper understanding of your own perception of your strengths versus how others perceive your strengths. Chapter one uses the Leadership Circle Profile assessment tool as the foundation for leadership competencies. As an emerging leader, we recommend that you first gain a strong understanding of your strengths. After you discern your strengths independently using the assessments referenced below, you may then want to consider taking a 360 degree assessment in which subordinates, peers, and supervisors evaluate your competencies. The 360 degree assessment is most appropriate after you have been managing people for a few years and are looking for feedback on your leadership and management skills.

Understanding your strengths is the first step to greater self-awareness and a better understanding of how to capitalize on your natural talents and abilities. Grounded in Positive Psychology, strengths-based approaches provide leaders with important perspectives for working in teams and groups, and the tools to engage in meaningful, positive application of their personal strengths. By learning how to capitalize on their own individual strengths and the strengths of others, emerging leaders learn the importance of building a diverse team, appreciating the contributions of team members, and the art of delegating for overall team success.

We recommend the Clifton StrengthsFinder, based on the culmination of more than 50 years of Dr. Donald O. Clifton's lifelong work that led millions of people around the world to discover their strengths. According to Gallup research, the thirty-four Clifton StrengthsFinder themes naturally cluster into four domains of leadership strength. The assessment identifies your top five themes and sorts them into the four domains (executing, influencing, relationship building, and strategic thinking). This information is very helpful as you think about how you can contribute to a team and who you need to surround yourself with.

To learn more about this strengths-based approach to leadership success, visit the Strengths.Gallup Web site and select the book Strengths-Based Leadership. The book you purchase will contain a unique access code that allows you to take the on-line assessment at no additional charge.

Because this assessment is based on positive psychology, it will help you see your strengths more clearly and will challenge you to view leadership from this new paradigm of appreciation; and in turn, provide you with a solid foundation to build upon. By design, it does not, however, provide insight into your weaknesses. Strengths-based approaches to leadership support the philosophy that you should FOCUS on your strengths and MANAGE your weaknesses. The better way to handle weakness is to surround yourself with people who are naturally talented in the areas where you are lacking in strength or to capitalize on your strengths when you encounter stumbling blocks along the way.

TABLE 4-1: MICROMANAGEMENT ASSESSMENT

		Usually	Often	Sometimes	Seldom	Almost Never
1	I review work with my employees to ensure quality					
2	I need to show my employees how their work should be done					
3	I try to track when my employees come and go					
4	I find myself having unscheduled status meetings with my employees					
5	I give my employees the responsibility to complete their work, but the authority for final decisions rests with me					
6	I require my employees to generate interim progress reports					
7	I find myself overruling the decisions of my employees					
8	I check on my employees' calendars to ensure that they are working on the correct projects					
9	I need to go beyond helping my employees prioritize their work, I need to prescribe 'the what' and 'the when' for them					
	Scoring					

		Usually	Often	Sometimes	Seldom	Almost Never
10	My employees know and are comfortable with what is expected of them					
11	My employees have all of the tools they need to complete their work					
12	My employees spend most of their time doing work that plays to their strengths					
13	I compliment my employees on their accomplishments at least once a week, every week					
14	I know my employees personally and talk with them freely about their personal lives					
15	I have at least quarterly discussions with my employees about their professional or career development					
16	My employees know that if they feel something is important, their voice will be heard; and if there is something important to know, they will hear it from me					
17	My employees feel that the mission of our company is important and that their work directly helps us accomplish that mission					
18	Employees believe their coworkers are doing quality work					
19	I talk with my employees about their progress toward their performance goals at least twice a year					
20	I have my employees engaged in a program of professional development that they find compelling					
	Scoring					

Scoring the Document

- ▰ Usually = 3 points
- ▰ Often = 2 points
- ▰ Sometimes = 1 point
- ▰ Seldom = 0 points
- ▰ Almost Never = 0 points

It is also recommended that you ensure that your leadership role does not require that you operate from an area of lesser strength the majority of the time. Research on strengths has shown that the highest achievers in a variety of fields: 1) operate the majority of the time from an area of strength; 2) have learned to partner or delegate to compensate for areas that are not their strength; 3) capitalize on their strengths in new situations; and 4) use their strengths to overcome obstacles.

- **Micromanagement Assessment** developed by Mike Morrow-Fox. This tool helps you determine that you are using the proper level of management versus micromanaging. Score yourself based on the specifics of your organization

Any management activity, when used on occasion, can be appropriate, appreciated, and engaging. When an employee is copying the president of the company on an e-mail, most employees appreciate a second set of eyes. Everyday management, however, respects the creative and evolving talents of the general workforce. Managers who find they regularly 'help' their employees complete their routine job functions rob those employees of professional growth opportunities that eventually impact organizational performance.

As such, *a score of 12 points or more on questions 1 through 9* indicate the likelihood that the manager is micromanaging. The higher the score above 12 on the first 9 questions, the greater the likelihood that employees feel stifled and find limited opportunities for professional growth.

Conversely, the final eleven questions relate to Gallup research on employee engagement. Engaged employees are more loyal, more productive, and more fulfilled than their neutral or disengaged counterparts. *A score of 22 or higher on questions 10 through 20* indicate that the manager is working toward engaging his employees. The higher the number exceeding 22, the greater the likelihood that the manager's employees feel engaged in their work.

Is it possible to have high scores on both sections of the inventory? Yes. What is likely to have happened, however, is that the manager taking the inventory is either giving his employees more latitude to work than he has indicated on the first part of the inventory, or that the manager may have overstated how engaged the employees feel on the second part of the inventory. It is very rare to find instances where employees are both micromanaged and engaged.

It is very helpful to take multiple assessments during the same period of time to paint a more complete and accurate picture of who you are as a leader. For example, the Enneagram shows your personality type; the MAP shows your ability to take multiple perspectives associated with levels of development; and the LCP shows how you are perceived by others, as well as how you see yourself. The combined or integrated assessment allows you to better understand your innate skills and abilities as well as your opportunities. This comprehensive information allows you to determine how you fit within your organization. Keep in mind that interpreting the data from these and other assessments often requires specialized expertise; we strongly recommend working with a certified coach. Similar to getting medical tests, the potential value of the information is only realized with proper translation.

Having a coach interpret the series of assessments as the foundation for your development plan can significantly increase your success since you will know exactly where to focus your efforts.

Now that we have presented four different types of assessments, you will have the opportunity to select the ones you are moved to take and consider how best to utilize the results.

Future Projections

We find that reading futurist publications in specific industries is helpful. The role of the futurist is to evaluate current trends and build possible scenarios for how the future might unfold. By building on your capacities for leadership, you can use these scenarios as part of your planning process to provide insight into overall societal trends, ensure that you are well prepared for the potential impact of ever-changing business conditions, and suggest imminent scenarios that help you navigate those trends effectively.

There are several organizations providing very effective views into the future. One that we regularly reference is The Arlington Institute (TAI), founded in 1989 by futurist John L. Petersen. It is a nonprofit research institute that specializes in thinking about global futures and creating conditions to influence rapid, positive change. They encourage systemic, non-linear approaches to planning and believe that effective thinking about the future is enhanced by applying emerging technology. TAI strives to be an effective agent of advancement by creating intellectual frameworks and toolsets for understanding the transition in which we are living.

Tools and Exercises

Now that you have reviewed the tools and taken some or all of the assessments, it is time to synthesize what you have learned about yourself through a Strengths, Weaknesses, Opportunities, and Threats worksheet (SWOT) and through a series of reflection questions. For the SWOT analysis, please complete the worksheet on the following page.

TABLE 4-2: SWOT ANALYSIS

Strengths	Opportunities
What sets you apart from most other people?	*What opportunities are open to those who have these strengths?*
Weaknesses	**Threats**
What do you need to improve?	*Do you have weaknesses that need to be addressed before you can move forward? Do any pose an immediate threat like losing your job?*

Development Journey Continued

Demetrius and Jonathan will now walk through their worksheets and journal entries for analyzing their individual situation and strengths.

DEMETRIUS'S SWOT WORKSHEET ANSWERS

Strengths

What sets you apart from most other people?

The thing that sets me apart from most people is my ability to think and work in a non-linear fashion and instead see things as three-dimensional. This helps me to assess a situation quickly to determine its validity or its ramifications and, thus, make a decision that is fully thought through in a matter of moments.

Opportunities

What opportunities are open to those who have these strengths?

This strength manifests as foresight and enables a leader to lead with a higher degree of certainty in a world that is full of uncertainty. Having the ability to quickly understand the impact of decisions that affect the viability of a company is an important leadership skill. More importantly, when making those decisions, having the confidence to stand firmly behind them, and then instilling the vision into the company for them to follow the direction with a high level of trust is invaluable.

Weaknesses

What do you need to improve?

I tend to wear my emotions on my sleeve when I am in strong disagreement. Over the years I have learned to keep my emotions in check, but I believe I have a long way to go until I have mastered the art of not being overly frustrated.

Threats

Do you have weaknesses that need to be addressed before you can move forward? Do any pose an immediate threat like losing your job?

I easily become bored if I do the same thing over and over, and if I am not stimulated or challenged enough. I'm big on constant growth and growth through learning. Once I have learned a new skill or conquered a new challenge, I like to move on. Dwelling on one thing in particular is a waste of time to me. At this point this weakness does not directly pose a threat to my job, but if the challenge I experience day-to-day begins to dwindle and the opportunities for continued growth disappear, I don't need to worry about losing my job because I will already be looking to fulfill my needs elsewhere.

JONATHAN'S SWOT WORKSHEET ANSWERS

Strengths	Opportunities
What sets you apart from most other people? I am able to identify opportunities before most other people, and to create a vision around these opportunities. I am also capable of inspiring others to join me in working toward that vision. A big part of this is being able to connect with a broad range of people and get them to agree on high-level items.	*What opportunities are open to those who have these strengths?* Those who have these strengths are able to locate and capitalize upon opportunities, and to build cohesive teams that can make a positive impact.
Weaknesses	**Threats**
What do you need to improve? I need to improve my ability to let go of things that are not important, and to accept that things are not going to be perfect and organized at all times. Additionally, I need to improve my attention to details on the things that do matter.	*Do you have weaknesses that need to be addressed before you can move forward? Do any pose an immediate threat like losing your job?* My desire for perfection and organization sometimes can steal some of my attention from the things that matter, so I need to make sure that I am balancing my drive with some time to ideate. Also, my inattention to some details of important things can cause inconveniences both for me and my teammates, so I need to make sure that I determine which details are important and not let them slip.

Innovative Leadership Reflection Questions

To help you develop your action plan, it is time to further clarify your direction using reflection questions. The questions for "What do I think/believe?" reflect your intentions. "What do I do?" questions reflect your actions. The questions "What do we believe?" reflect the culture of your organization (i.e. work, school, community), and "How do we do this?" questions reflect systems and processes for your organization. This exercise is an opportunity to practice innovative leadership by considering your vision for yourself and how it will play out in the context of your life. You will define your intentions, actions, culture, and systems in a systematic manner.

Table 4-2 contains an exhaustive list of questions to appeal to a broad range of readers. Find a few that fit your own personal situation; focus on the questions that seem the most relevant. We recommend you answer one to three questions from each category.

TABLE 4-3: REFLECTION QUESTIONS

What do I think/believe?

- Given the direction the world is moving, how do you believe you are positioned to be a leader in the future?

- Are you able to balance professional and personal commitments? How does your leadership style impact your ability to meet your overall life goals?

- How has your leadership style contributed to the organization's success? Have you done things that did not produce the results you had hoped? How would you change to produce different results?

- How would you like to impact the people who work for you? Have they grown and met their career goals while working for you? What have they contributed to the organization while working for you?

What do I do?

- How do you play to your strengths?

- How do you mitigate the threats?

- How do you take advantage of opportunities?

- How do you compensate for weaknesses?

- What assessments are you taking to gather objective data about your performance? This could include performance appraisals, developmental assessments, 360° feedback, or informal feedback from multiple sources.

- How do you appropriately respond to your personal sense of urgency while supporting organizational objectives?

- What messages do you convey that use emotion, external expert sources, and sense of clarity to demonstrate urgency?

- How do you communicate your personal changes and your sense of urgency to those around you who may be impacted?

What do we believe?

- Notice the various people and groups in your life (family, colleagues, boss, community, friends, etc.) and what they report as "urgent."

- Anticipate how they will interpret your change. How will they talk about it? Specifically for your organization, how will the changes you aspire to make impact your constituents?

- Determine how your sense of urgency connects with the group's sense of urgency based on its priorities, goals, and pain points.

- How does the culture of your support system impact your beliefs about yourself and about leadership? Would these beliefs change if you changed who you spent time with?

- Based on developmental perspectives, where is the cultural center of gravity in your support system? How are people with more open perspectives perceived?

- What are the cultural barriers impeding your changes? What are the cultural enablers? Will your changes be aligned with the organizational culture? Will they send a message that you do not value the culture?

<table>

> **How do we do this?**
>
> - What systems and processes are enablers or barriers that will impact my development?
> - What processes and measures alert us to urgency in our system that we need to tend to? What are the early warning signs?
> - What processes measure your progress? Are you progressing as measured by criteria that will increase your professional effectiveness? Are you progressing against your personal standards? How will your support system or organization reward or punish your changes based on the measures?
> - Do the measures indicate a sense of urgency to you that support focusing on development?

Demetrius's Reflection Responses

We will now walk through Demetrius's answers to one or two questions from each section of Table 4-3. Simply follow along with Demetrius to answer the questions for yourself, or select questions that fit your current situation.

What do I think/believe?

- *Do you need to change to accomplish your goals? Is the change in perspective or expanded capabilities at the same level?*

   I absolutely need to change in order to achieve my goals. When I think back to my time as an undergraduate preparing to enter the "real world," I knew I had to change. Even then, I knew I needed to address situations in a more mature manner, to seek additional skills by virtue of independent studies, and to embrace the notion of being an adult. Now looking to my future and the goals I have set forth, I realize I must change once again. If I plan to be an entrepreneur, I need to change my perception of the things I dread doing and instead understand that this discomfort is part of what I am signing up for in to become a successful entrepreneur. I also understand that I need to expand my approach to communication. I'm very comfortable and competent talking about a broad range of topics, but don't necessarily like to sell my abilities. To paraphrase the adage about action versus words, I much prefer that my work shows what I'm capable of, instead of telling someone what I'm capable of. However, as an entrepreneur I know I must improve my ability to communicate the depth of my skill set to others.

- *How would you like to impact the people who work for you? Have they grown and met their career goals while working for you? What have they contributed to the organization while working for you?*

   I have always believed the best way to lead after setting the course is to simply stay out of the way and, when necessary, make a few course corrections to ensure the end goal is still in sight. I adopted this approach as the leader of a team that went to a client site and was asked to deliver the product at a given time on my first assignment. I took this as an opportunity to try several techniques I had studied over the previous few years. One such technique was to allow the team more freedom. We all had an understanding of the end goal and the milestones that needed to be achieved along the way. Throughout the course of this particular day, if a team member needed to leave the office to complete a personal task, she was given the flexibility to prioritize her workload with the understanding that the timeline to deliver at the client site must still be met within the designated time frame. This sense of freedom enabled the team to attend to aspects of their personal lives that could only be addressed during core working hours while entrusting them with the accountability to complete the necessary work within the specified time frame. The results were that members of the team were happy, the product delivered to the client was of high quality, and we were asked to take on even more at the client site.

Using this method of leadership, I now work with each member of the team on my current projects to help them determine their short- and long-term career goals. I have set aside a chunk of time for each member of the team during the project to work on self-improvement and to determine what they need from me in order to achieve their goals.

What do I do?

- *How do you model appropriate responses for the sense of urgency in personal actions that are true for you while supporting organizational objectives?*

I have found that the best way to address my personal sense of urgency while supporting organizational objectives is to continuously deliver results. I find that it's really easy to criticize or question my work approach or methods when not delivering on the objectives of the organization. However, no matter how unorthodox the method may be, if the objectives are being met, and to a large extent surpassed, the approach or method no longer comes into question as long as we are working within the organization's guiding principles.

What do we believe?

- *How does the culture of your support system impact your belief about yourself and about leadership? Would these beliefs change if you changed who you spend time with?*

There is a theory that you are the average of your five closest friends—which seems important since my friends create a sense of community in my life. I first heard about this theory in 2002, and decided to see if it held true. It did. Now looking at the culture of my support system and my five closest friends and how they impact my leadership, I have to say they have little impact on my leadership. My leadership methods come from the books I've read or the training I've received as a function of increasing my effectiveness at my place of employment.

I can see this belief about leadership changing as a function of with whom I spend my time, but only with regard to the people I spend time with at work or at networking events. I tend to find I pick up invaluable nuggets of information at the networking events that I can then integrate directly into my leadership methods at work.

Now that I am enrolled in an MBA program, I have also used courses as a valuable way to learn more about leadership and test my ideas with people I respect within that group.

■ *Determine how your sense of urgency connects with the group's sense of urgency based on their priorities, goals, and pain points.*

Some of my peers are going through the MBA program at a leisurely pace, while others are stretching the program out because their employers are paying for the degree. I've found that my sense of urgency is different than the sense of urgency of the group of students with whom I started the program. The reason is that I have accelerated the rate at which I'm going through the program so that I can spend more time with my daughter. For me, family is a value that I hold near and dear, and being able to spend time with my daughter as she grows is of the utmost importance to me. I simply want to finish the program as soon as possible no matter how much stress that may put on me.

How do we do this?

■ *What systems and processes are enablers or barriers that will impact my development?*

The biggest barrier that may impact my development is me. Time and time again I have proven that when I make up my mind to accomplish a goal, I tend to achieve it. An issue I have run into in the past is that I am sometimes in conflict over which path I would like to take, and time passes before I truly make up my mind. I need to be consistent and decisive with regard to my behavior in all aspects of my life to ensure I can overcome all barriers.

Jonathan's Responses to Reflection Questions

We'll now walk through Jonathan's answers to one or two questions from each section of Table 4-2. Simply follow along with Jonathan to answer the questions for yourself, or select question that fit your current situation.

What do I think/believe?

- *Given the direction the world is moving, do you believe you are positioned to be a leader in the future?*

  I believe that I am positioned to be a vision-based leader; that is, a leader who creates, champions, envisions, and gets people on board with that vision. This type of leadership is best actualized in collaboration with detail- and technology-focused leaders who can help me to implement my vision within my organization on more detailed levels.

What do I do?

- *How do you play to your strengths?*

  I know what I am good at, as does my team, and these are the things that I am responsible for. The inverse is true for my weaknesses. Having a good discussion with a team to analyze each person's strengths and weaknesses is a good way to know these things and act on them going forward. There are, however, always opportunities to grow into new responsibilities and let go of outdated ones.

What do we believe?

- *How does the culture of your support system impact your beliefs about yourself and about leadership? Would these beliefs change if you changed who you spent time with?*

  We always view ourselves differently when we are around different types of people. I may come off incredibly aggressive in front of one person, whereas perceived as less aggressive in front of another. It is very important not to judge the quality of our leadership and the progress of our improvement through the eyes of just one other person. That is why having multiple personal mentors is so important—collectively this group can help me improve in ways that only one mentor or colleague could not.

How do we do this?

- *What systems and processes are enablers and barriers that will impact my development?*

  Time commitment and responsibility are two large barriers to my development. Being able to completely step away from work once in a while is very important to breaking down these barriers and getting a chance to grow. To ensure I do step away from work, I schedule time with friends at least once a month and time to recharge by myself at least once a week. Another key enabler in development is the people with whom I surround myself, including my personal mentors, friends, and colleagues. They can help to recommend areas and mechanisms for improvement, and they can keep me accountable to following through on improving ourselves. I schedule conversations weekly with one supportive person ranging from family to mentors to colleagues. Tending to the important relationships in my life ensures I can call on them any time. The combination of scheduling activities to get away from work and maintaining and building a strong support network allow me to remain strong and resilient.

Your Process of Evaluating Your Situation and Strengths

Now that you have followed Demetrius and Jonathan's responses, it is time to complete the worksheets. Based on your assessment results, if you have not done so already, complete the SWOT analysis in Table 4-2 and answer one to three questions from each section in Table 4-3 for yourself. By internalizing your strengths and opportunities, you can identify the gaps that, when filled, will help you to accomplish your vision. Understanding your weaknesses will also help you know what to avoid, what to improve, and what personal feedback to request from people skilled in those areas.

We encourage you to complete all of the exercises, taking your time and giving proper attention to gathering input from several different sources. When you have a clear picture of your strengths and opportunities, you will be ready to move to the next step. You may now find that you have a different or clearer perception about where you excel, and how those areas can complement your vision.

This chapter helped you clarify your strengths and weaknesses as a foundation for your personal transformation journey. Bear in mind that you are creating your own story through this process. The next chapter focuses on the framework for creating a development plan that will allow you to close the gap between your vision and where you are today.

Resources

- **Enneagram:** www.enneagraminstitute.com

- **Mature Adult Profile Assessment (MAP):** www.pacificintegral.com

- **The Leadership Circle 360° Assessment:** www.theleadershipcircle.com

- **Resilience Assessment:** www.metcalf-associates.com

- **Overall Innovative Leadership Assessment:** www.metcalf-associates.com

- **Susanne Cook-Greuter research:** www.cook-greuter.com

- **Leadership Agility 360:** www.changewise.biz

- **StrengthsFinder:** www.strengthsfinder.com

What do I think/believe?

What do I do?

What do we believe?

How do we do this?

CHAPTER 5

Step 3: Plan Your Journey

When you have a solid plan for your development journey, you begin investing your time and energy based on your vision, your strengths and weaknesses, and your development goals. In order to stay motivated, it is important to experience a sense of measurable growth. Tangible results are especially crucial to implementing change, and demonstrating progress is naturally part of the expectation. An example is: If my boss wants me to show that I am a good leader before he will promote me, I need to show that I am "good" as measured by the boss's criteria. So, in this case, I would want to understand the criteria as well as know what the boss values, and build a plan that allows me to show those results. On the other hand, if I am developing for my own personal growth, I may not be as concerned about showing results to others, but will still want to feel I am making progress.

As you can imagine, some results will take longer than others to manifest. Our experience with clients has shown that leaders can certainly make quick progress in some areas, but progress in other areas may take years.

Your life situation will also impact your development. For example, a leader may be a great provider for his family, and this is a core value he holds. He might create meaningful results that help cultivate developmental growth by focusing on specific behaviors that will promote his well-being and success. In other words, he may simply experience a sense of progress ranging from a greater feeling of calm, clearer thinking, and better relationships with colleagues which will lead to better performance. He may also see measured results quantitatively using a 360° assessment (gaining feedback from several stakeholder groups at multiple levels within the organization including boss, peers, and subordinates) showing significant improvements in key leadership-related qualities. Another leader who wants to have a greater impact on the world may have an entirely different development focus and plan.

Consider the value of investing your energy in this journey as a way to foster meaningful change for the people closest to you. If you know, for example, that you have specific behaviors that are particularly difficult for your boss, an important colleague, or a loved one, you may want to prioritize those areas for improvement.

Options Development Plan Focus

As you begin building your capacity, you may want to consider two distinct, yet essential, areas, external capacity and internal capacity. Though the research emphasizing the importance of both is compelling, most of our formal training still focuses on hard skills (external capabilities). This exclusive emphasis leaves many leaders ill-prepared for, and in some cases uninformed about, the importance of internal capacity, such as emotional intelligence and interpersonal skills. Research among Fortune 500 companies at Stanford University showed that 90% of those who failed as leaders did so because they lacked the interpersonal skills that are a critical component of emotional intelligence. This is confirmed by research conducted by the Center for Creative Leadership finding that poor interpersonal skills are a leading cause of derailment from executive-level positions. These terms are defined as:

- **External capacity (hard skills)** – Skills and behaviors associated with professional success. This is where most professional development efforts have been focused.

- **Internal capacity** – Includes intention, world view, purpose, vision, values, cultural norms, emotional stability, resilience, a sense of being grounded, overall personal well-being, intuition, balanced perspective, and attitude, and serves as the foundation for you to accomplish your deepest aspirations. Internal capacity is also required to move on to later stages of development.

To accomplish your vision, you may benefit from one or all of the following three developmental focuses:

- **Becoming more effective; developing new skills and/or behaviors** – Changing behaviors and building skills that will significantly impact performance, as measured by observed behavioral change. As you advance in your job responsibilities and/or as the organizational environment changes, you will continually need to build new skills. These can range from an understanding of how to leverage social media to promote your organization to building a board. In this category, the focus is on skills that can be developed through training programs.

- **Building on your current strengths** – Development can take the form of focusing on enhancing current strengths. It can also focus on important behaviors that adversely impact success. Again, we recommend focusing 80% of your effort toward building on your passions and the other 20% toward shoring up your deficiencies. This is a general recommendation; it is important to remember that your specific situation and needs will be clear indicators of what changes are required for your continued growth and success.

- **Minimizing your weaknesses** – In the Strengths, Weaknesses, Opportunities, and Threats (SWOT) analysis, you may have identified some behaviors that impede further growth. These may have been behaviors that made you successful in your current development (sometimes referred to as overused strengths). Even so, part of your development is examining the events and behaviors that got you here and understanding which interfere with your success as defined by your vision. For example, you may identify yourself as someone who is on top of every task. As your responsibilities grow, you will delegate more, but you may still feel uncomfortable with your lack of knowledge of the details. Trying to manage the details to the level that made you successful will become a weakness as you move up. It is important to tend to these behavioral changes as part of your plan. The challenge here may be shifting the focus away from daily details toward strategic thinking and expanding your ability beyond one or a few core strengths to develop several additional capabilities.

In most organizations, the vast majority of development efforts focus on hard skills (including advanced degrees and certification programs), and thus, many leaders need to balance them by explicitly exercising internal capacity. To further describe this process, we use the term mastery, which simply means the capacity to not only produce results, but also to master the principles underlying those results. In other words, as a master, you can deliver results comfortably due to the internal capacity behind your skills and judgment.

Personal mastery involves enhancing your internal capacity to support the skills you have acquired while also removing barriers to your success. To help you achieve personal mastery, we recommend you enrich your ongoing development plan and personal practices (activities we repeat until we master them, like our golf swing).

There are some important factors to consider when creating your plan. First, just as in physical training, you will get more leverage if you cross-train or develop several areas at the same time. According to Ken Wilber (AQAL Framework), there are benefits to cross-training beyond simply focusing on one area. For example, people who both lift weights and meditate tend to make greater improvements in both areas than those who do one or the other. Evidence suggests that a combination of activities from different parts of our lives complement one another. This is quite true in the leadership arena as well.

A comprehensive plan will take into consideration each of the dimensions that are foundational to the human experience: physical, emotional, mental, and spiritual (people not comfortable with the term *spiritual* can substitute *altruistic* or *purpose*). If any of these elements are neglected, you are likely to find it will adversely impact your success in other areas over the long term.

There are standard programs designed to help this process. One of the programs we suggest is Integral Transformative Practice (ITP), developed by Michael Murphy and George Leonard. This practice involves a strong cross-training routine. Nine commitments form the essential building blocks of the ITP program. They create the roadmap for practitioners to follow to realize their potential through the cross-training of body, mind, heart, and soul. The commitments include aerobic exercise, mindful eating, strength training, staying emotionally current, a service component, and the ITP Kata, which is a 40-minute series involving movements derived from yoga and Aikido, deep relaxation techniques, imagery, affirmations, and meditation. ITP is a long-term program for realizing the potential of body (exercise), mind (reading, discussion), heart (staying emotionally current, community), and soul (meditation, affirmations). Joining a local ITP group can augment a strong individual practice.

Tools and Exercises

The range of tools is quite broad, so it is important to select something that feels safe and consistent with your values. The objective is to create a plan that you can follow and stick with to accomplish your goals. To help you get started, we put suggestions in Table 5-1. While several items fall within multiple categories, we attempted to classify them to be as mutually exclusive as possible. Some activities will provide benefits across several categories. An example of this is meditation, as it can help you manage your negative thinking, improve focus, balance emotions, and improve decision-making capacity.

Healthy development encompasses work in all areas. The practices you choose may evolve, and your practice may also fluctuate based on other life demands. We encourage you to maintain as much consistency as possible. Just as the benefit of exercise increases when you hit a specific frequency and duration, the same will be true for leadership development practices. The more you invest, the better your results will be.

TABLE 5-1: RECOMMENDATIONS FOR INTERNAL AND EXTERNAL CAPACITY BUILDING - ACTIVITIES TO CONSIDER INCORPORATING INTO PLAN

What activities can I do to impact my internal capacity (what I think and believe)?

- Spirit
  - Define vision
  - Define values
  - Pray
  - Participate in religious practices
  - Religious study
  - Seek spiritual counseling
  - Seek a spiritual teacher
  - Visualize goals
  - Become socially active – volunteer
- Ethics
  - Create guiding principles or values
  - Pay attention to ethics around you
  - Address situations you find unethical
  - Read and learn about ethics

- Emotions (Emotional Quotient)
  - Meditate
  - Seek therapy
  - Practice HeartMath techniques
  - Practice shadow exercises - the ability to find in yourself the things you find frustrating in others and address them as growth opportunities
  - Keep a journal
  - Seek coaching
  - Maintain strong friendships

What activities can I do to impact my external capacity?

- Body
  - Exercise
  - Yoga
  - Relaxation
  - Weight lifting
  - Mindful eating/healthy diet
  - Sufficient sleep
- Cross Training
  - Integral Transformative Practice (yoga, aikido, relaxation, visualization, meditation)
  - Reflection practices (do-reflect-learn)

- Mind
  - Read
  - Study
  - Attend lectures and discussion groups
  - Attend school
  - Perspective-taking exercises
  - Take stretch assignments
  - Volunteer for opportunities to build skills (charity work)
  - Manage polarities
  - Action inquiry
  - Mindfulness-Based Stress reduction

What activities can I do that impact us as a group (what we think/believe)?

- Review the list above and determine which activities can be completed in a group. What groups do I participate in, and do they have similar values?
- Develop a mission and values as a family. You may choose to set family meditation time or gym time to promote a family sense of focus and well-being. Many families share religious traditions and find that they provide a solid foundation and a shared set of values

What structures and/or groups will help? What groups or programs do I participate in?

- Family activities could include how we eat, our exercise routines, our family reading time, our church or spiritual practice, and our volunteer activities
- Friend/social activities include what I do with my friends that support and that hinder my development, such as exercise groups, emotional support, honest and accurate feedback, and dialogue practices
- Work events and support, including yoga classes, weight management support, fitness classes, insurance discounts for fitness, and smoking cessation programs
- Practice groups for development, such as Integral Transformative Practice, meditation, and church
- Study groups
- Formal education programs
- Informal education programs
- Fitness groups and programs, such as running clubs, ski clubs, exercise groups, and gym memberships

The following is a development plan template designed to help you create a plan that allows you achieve your goals. This table focuses mainly on identifying opportunities and the intentions behind your desire to change.

TABLE 5-2: SKILL/BEHAVIOR DEVELOPMENT WORKSHEET Evaluate and Select Skill/Behavioral Change Priorities – Worksheet		
Key Actions	**Detailed Action Planning**	**Behavior 1**
Select behaviors	Which behaviors do I want to improve or change? Which behaviors do I perform well that I would like to enhance?	
What are the consequences of this behavior?	What will happen if I continue to demonstrate this behavior in the future? How will my service recipients be impacted? How will my career be impacted? How will my colleagues be impacted? How will my organization be impacted?	
Why do I demonstrate this behavior?	I have developed behaviors over the course of my life because they made sense. What has changed to make this behavior ineffective now?	
How would I like to perform in the future?	Write an end-result statement describing the changes I will make and the impact of those changes. What will an observer see when I have made these changes?	
Who will help me change?	Who could I ask to provide me with feedback on how I am doing? Who could be a good mentor?	
What type of support do I want?	Make an agreement with a person I trust about how I would like us to support one another in changing behaviors. How will that person hold me accountable for taking this step? How will I support him in changing his behavior? Is there a group that will support me in the long term?	
What will I do or not do?	What other actions could I take? What am I willing to commit to doing? What am I committed to stopping?	
When will I complete actions?	When will I have completed action items?	

TABLE 5-2: SKILL/BEHAVIOR DEVELOPMENT WORKSHEET
Evaluate and Select Skill/Behavioral Change Priorities – Jonathan's Example

Key Actions	Detailed Action Planning	Behavior 1
Select behaviors	Which behaviors do I want to improve or change? Which behaviors do I perform well that I would like to enhance?	Improve/change letting go of unimportant issues; increasing attention to important details Enhance: identifying opportunities; building vision and commitment behind it
What are the consequences of this behavior?	What will happen if I continue to demonstrate this behavior in the future? How will my service recipients be impacted? How will my career be impacted? How will my colleagues be impacted? How will my organization be impacted?	I will continue to be stressed when I should not be, and will create stress for others as well Enhance: I will continue to build movements and organizations that matter to people, and give others the opportunity to take part
Why do I demonstrate this behavior?	I have developed behaviors over the course of my life because they made sense. What has changed to make this behavior ineffective now?	I have extremely high standards for myself and for others Enhance: I follow my heart and do what I love
How would I like to perform in the future?	Write an end-result statement describing the changes I will make and the impact of those changes. What will an observer see when I have made these changes?	I no longer worry about insignificant things, so I am instead able to focus my energy on important details Enhance: To accomplish my vision, I have multiple projects going at once, that are well-staffed by people I trust
Who will help me change?	Who could I ask to provide me with feedback on how I am doing? Who could be a good mentor?	My community of personal mentors will help me, as will my family members and colleagues
What type of support do I want?	Make an agreement with a person I trust about how I would like us to support one another in changing behaviors. How will that person hold me accountable for taking this step? How will I support him in changing his behavior? Is there a group that will support me in the long term?	I will lay out my needs to my personal mentors, and ask that they help me by making these needs the first point of conversation in all meetings that we have
What will I do or not do?	What other actions could I take? What am I willing to commit to doing? What am I committed to stopping?	I will continue working my same job, but will be doing a daily self-examination and a weekly mentor meeting to track my progress on meeting my goals to change. I am committed to stop getting stressed about insignificant things, and to pay attention to the details that matter
When will I complete actions?	When will I have completed action items?	Using the weekly mentoring and daily routine described above, I will complete my goal of improving upon my weaknesses in 4 months. I will complete my goal of improving upon my strengths in one year, using the same method

The next template was designed to synthesize development activities reflected in the prior worksheets.

We recommend that all goals be SMART, an acronym by George T. Doran referenced in the November 1981 issue of *Management Review*. SMART goals comprise five characteristics:

- **Specific** - Goals should be definitive and clearly defined. When goals are specific, it is clear to see when they are reached. To make goals specific, they must clarify exactly what is expected, why it is important, who's involved, where it is going to happen. *Overall example of a goal: Teachers want to improve the reading levels of all the children in their program by 25% in one school year to ensure their future academic success.*

- **Measurable** - Establish concrete criteria for measuring progress toward the attainment of each goal you set. Measurable defines what and how much change you are expecting. *Example: 25% in one school year is the measurement.*

- **Attainable** - When you identify goals that are most important to you, you begin to figure out ways you can make them come true. You develop the attitudes, abilities, skills, and financial capacity to reach them. You begin seeing previously overlooked opportunities to bring yourself closer to the achievement of your goals. "Attainable" ensures that your expectations are reasonable. *Example: One school year and 25% are reasonable goals; 80% in one semester is not an attainable goal.*

- **Realistic** - To be realistic, a goal must represent an objective toward which you are both willing and able to work. A goal can be both high and realistic. You are the only one who can decide the height of your goal, but be sure that every goal represents substantial progress. "Realistic" ensures you have the capacity to meet your goal. *Example: 25% is realistic— children can improve that percentage in a year.*

- **Timely** - A goal should be grounded within an approximate time frame. Goals lacking time frames also lack urgency. Being timely ensures you have a deadline to meet your goals. As Dan Heath and Chip Heath state in *Switch: How to Change Things When Change is Hard*, "Some is not a number. Soon is not a time." *Example: One school year is a defined period of time.*

Using the information from the worksheets and templates provided, you are now ready to complete your Development Planning Worksheet. This worksheet will serve as the foundation for the actions you will take to accomplish your goals, and should reflect your data gathering in the assessment chapter and your personal reflection.

TABLE 5-3: DEVELOPMENT PLANNING WORKSHEET
Development Planning Worksheet

Current State	Future State/Goal	Actions	By When?	Measure - How do you know?

Development Plan Continued

DEVELOPMENT PLANNING WORKSHEET – JONATHAN'S EXAMPLE				
Current State	**Future State/ Goal**	**Actions**	**By When?**	**Measurement – How do you know?**
Have a difficult time letting go of imperfection and insignificant details	Able to let go of things that do not matter and quickly take action on details that do matter	Daily routine of self-examination of how well I am doing in meeting this goal; weekly meeting with a personal mentor who is aware of my goal	Four months from today	On a weekly basis: How many nights am I coming home in a stressed mood? How many times am I making a mistake that affects me and at least one other person?
Skilled at identifying opportunities, creating a vision around them, and building a coalition to support them	Able to identify multiple opportunities, create multiple projects, and build multiple teams within the same organization	Daily routine of recording opportunities that are in my mind, and defining a specific vision around each one; weekly meeting with a personal mentor to coach me in the art of balancing multiple projects	One year from today	By the number of high-quality projects I have going on in my organization, and how many committed people are working on each project

Demetrius's Developmental Journey Continued

Demetrius will now walk through his worksheets and journal entries for planning his journey. When we last met Demetrius he had completed analyzing his situation and strengths.

DEVELOPMENT PLANNING WORKSHEET – DEMETRIUS'S EXAMPLE				
Current State	**Future State/ Goal**	**Actions**	**By When?**	**Measurement – How do you know?**
I would like to start my own business focusing on leading and empowering, and not simply managing	◾ Have business up and running ◾ Continued growth in leadership	◾ Finish creating business plan ◾ Determine location for business ◾ Hire staff at all levels within the organization that believe leadership is necessary and that they play a role	Within the next three years	Company will exist Staff will work as a cohesive unit while focusing on personal growth
Improve overall health and physical ability	Become physically healthier	◾ Meditation ◾ Exercise regularly ◾ Mindful eating	Focus on these actions for the next nine months	Better year after year times for 5k events

Innovative Leadership Reflection Questions

To help you develop your action plan, it is time to further clarify your direction using reflection questions. The questions for "What do I think/believe?" reflect your intentions. "What do I do?" questions reflect your actions. The questions "What do we believe?" reflect the culture of your organization (i.e., work, school, community), and "How do we do this?" questions reflect systems and processes for your organization. This exercise is an opportunity to practice innovative leadership by considering your vision for yourself and how it will play out in the context of your life. You will define your intentions, actions, culture, and systems in a systematic manner.

Table 5-4 contains an exhaustive list of questions to appeal to a broad range of readers. You will likely find that a few of these best fit your own personal situation. Focus on the questions that seem the most relevant. We recommend you answer one to three questions from each of the categories.

TABLE 5-4: QUESTIONS TO GUIDE THE LEADER AND ORGANIZATION

What do I think/believe?

- What are my priorities for development? Are they reflected in the plan I created?
- Am I willing to make the changes necessary to meet my goals?
- What do I consider personal short-term wins?
- Which wins do I want to see in what time frame? Is this reasonable?
- What do I consider a win for my team?
- What do I consider a win for the organization?
- Which short-term wins will be really important to key people in my life?
- How do I stay motivated to work toward goals that will take a long time or a lifetime to accomplish? How will I think about life changes, such as changing eating habits versus dieting?
- Have I taken into account the whole range of activities I need to create a sustainable change, such as involving others and creating a plan that I can live with long term?

What do I do?

- How do I translate my vision into long and short-term goals?
- Are my goals SMART?
- What are my financial goals and milestones?
- Is this a plan that is sustainable in the long term? Will accomplishing my short-term wins motivate me to stay on track with my long-term plan?
- Does my plan contain the foundation work as well as skill building (example: basic health as well as business competencies)?
- Which wins can I identify and support that solve problems and are seeds for future shifts?
- Which changes in my behavior will demonstrate a strong statement to others and encourage their ongoing support, while possibly modeling changes that could also serve them?

What do we believe?

- Which wins will provide meaningful tangible and emotional results, and gain support of key stakeholders in my life?

- Which wins will encourage others to engage in their own personal/professional growth initiatives?

- Which stories can we tell others about the wins that were shared with the organization to encourage them to focus on their development?

- Which wins are reinforced by our culture and values? Which wins would be opposed to our culture and values?

How do we do this?

- How do I align my goals and short-term wins with the organization such that I receive support for the changes I am making? How do I ensure that early wins are important to key stakeholders?

- How do I track and measure my wins and their impact against overall personal and organizational goals? Do I have early warning measures?

- Are my wins aligned with the larger organizational objectives?

- Does the organization reinforce and reward the behavioral changes I am making?

- How will I connect my personal wins to the organizational vision and measures to demonstrate the impact of my small steps forward?

Demetrius's Reflection Responses

We will now walk through Demetrius's answers to one or two questions from each section of Table 5-4. Simply follow along with Demetrius to answer the questions for yourself or select the questions that fit your current situation.

What do I think/believe?

- *What are my priorities for development? Are they reflected in the plan I created?*

   Throughout my life I have always believed in the concept of "stepping stones" to each life goal. As an undergraduate computer science engineering student, I loved the logic and puzzles involved with creating computer software to solve everyday problems; however, I knew that I didn't want to be a programmer all of my life because I enjoy the interaction with people that most programmers shy away from. With that, I decided to focus on my soft skills so that I could communicate effectively with customers and individuals within the organization. So my next logical step was to obtain a professional certification in project management. This allowed me to still be involved in the software development process while expanding my communication opportunities.

   The next priority in my development was to better understand how businesses run and how they operate. To acquire this knowledge, I enrolled in the MBA program at Capital University. As I come closer to graduation, I feel fulfilled by the education I have obtained as it relates to my understanding of business, but I also feel I have learned more about myself that will help me as I continue to progress through the next steps of my life and my career.

■ *What do I consider a win for my team?*

Part of being an effective leader means providing opportunities for those you lead to grow toward their goals. For each project I manage, I always want to understand the areas of growth each team member would like to work on while part of my team, and throughout the project I provide them with every opportunity to achieve their goals. For example, one software developer on my team wanted to understand how to grow into the role of a business analyst (BA). Throughout the duration of our project, I teamed the developer with our most senior BA so she could see how the BA did her job. When the BA met with the client to understand the requirements, the developer sat in on those meetings so she could see firsthand the interaction and the methods employed by the BA. While this process is still ongoing, the door was opened and the developer has begun obtaining the necessary skills to make a career change.

So, what do I consider a win for my team? A win is when all members are working together for the good of each other while still delivering exceptional value as one team to our customer.

What do I do?

■ *How do I translate my vision into long- and short-term goals?*

When I plan my goals, I like to think of them in a more sequential pattern than I do other aspects of my life. I structure the majority of my short-term goals in a way that feeds my long-term goals—which are in direct correlation to the vision of how I see myself in the future. While I have to make course corrections along the way to ensure I am able to achieve each goal toward the realization of my vision, I also remove goals that no longer make sense.

For example, I have a clear vision in my head of spending time with my daughter at the park on a sunny day watching her learn and experience new things, and just enjoying every moment with her. When this particular vision was conceptualized, my long-term goal (only two years into the future from that time) was to complete the MBA program as quickly as possible and obtain the skills I felt would be important to my career. To achieve that goal, during my first semester on campus I mapped out every class I would need to take to meet the requirements for graduation while still meeting my reasons for going into the MBA program. Once that long-term goal was determined, I worked on my short-term goals.

My short-term goals were simple, take each semester one semester at a time and each week of the semester one week at a time. Taking this approach helped me to focus on the week at hand while understanding the bigger picture of the semester and without worrying about the length of the overall MBA program. Then, during the semesters in which I would need to take three classes—meaning I would be away three nights a week—I shifted focus back to my overall vision as a reminder that completing this goal meant that my vision would materialize even faster.

- *What are my financial goals and milestones?*

I recall while I was in high school that my financial goal was to make $50,000 a year. At the time I thought this was a large sum of money that would allow me to live within an upper-middle class lifestyle. The truth is, while this amount is far above the poverty line, my lifestyle vision and the dollar amount I associated with this vision didn't match, and I realized I didn't want to associate a dollar amount to my standard of living. With that said, my wife and I often reflect on our current living status and ask a few simple questions: are we in a situation in which we are living paycheck to paycheck? Are we in a situation in which we can comfortably go out and spend some disposable income without it negatively affecting the household? Are we able to set money aside for our future separate from the 401Ks that we have? Are we comfortable with our overall living arrangements? If the answers to these questions mean we do not need an immediate adjustment, then we are reaching our financial goals. However, the last item to consider is: do we see any changes in the short-term or long-term future that would necessitate making a change to our financial situation? As an example, the financial implications of having another baby would require us to reassess our financial situation to determine if our current financial state will support this change, and, if not, when and how do we begin to make adjustments?

What do we believe?

- *Which wins will encourage others to engage in their own personal and professional growth initiatives?*

I believe the wins that encourage others to engage in their own personal and professional growth initiatives are the ones that show the value for them personally or the added value to their end-customers. In a work environment, when you not only complete the work that you are there to complete, but also add a sense of value that was not expected, the customer wins. That win is the most important to the customer because you were expected to complete the assigned job—and the extra value is a bonus. That win is what they will talk about more and more, and that win is what makes them come back to you time and time again. From that standpoint, when outsiders see a customer's reaction to the added value you've provided, the question becomes "how can I do that?" and renders the opportunity for others to grow.

- *Which wins are reinforced by our culture and values? Which wins would be opposed to our culture and values?*

There is a huge difference between meeting a goal and achieving a win, and the terms are not interchangeable. Unfortunately, I believe we reinforce the goals more often than we reward a true win. When an organization only looks at the result of a win without examining the reasons for the win, then that organization is doomed to applaud the wrong behaviors that could have contributed to the win. For example, if a project came in under budget and early, and the organization applauded without knowing that the team members were treated horribly by the project manager and the customer was told what would be received, as opposed to being asked what was needed or wanted, then this is a bad win for the culture and the organizational values. I believe it's important to know why and how a win came about, to applaud the aspects that went well, and find ways to fix areas that didn't go so well. Within my team we conduct retrospectives every two weeks to answer these questions. This enables us to address and quickly fix things that are going wrong, as opposed to waiting until a project is complete—because at that point it's too late to make any significant change for that project.

How do we do this?

- *How do I align my goals and short-term wins with the organization such that I receive support for changes I am making? How do I ensure that early wins are important to key stakeholders?*

  In order to achieve this, it's important to understand in which direction the organization is headed and ensure that the changes you're making reinforce the goals of the organization. Like many other organizations, my organization believes it's important to be valued partners with our clients while providing them with top-of-the-line consulting services. I've used many tools that I have learned over the last five years to lead my team toward achieving the goals of our clients and our organization. Part of my goal is to put the things I have learned into practice while ensuring we continue to deliver exceptional results.

  The way I establish that the wins are important to the stakeholders is by consistent and effective communication to confirm that my team is on the same page as our client. In order to do this, I have to assure we are constantly communicating a client's needs, wants, and anything that may not be going right. Focusing my efforts in communication ensures that the win they receive is the one they are looking for.

Jonathan's Reflection Responses

We will now walk through Jonathan's answers to one or two questions from each section of Table 5-4.

What do I think/believe?

- *Which short-term wins will be really important to key people in my life?*

  The short-term wins that are most important to people in my life are the reduction of stress and improvement in my attention to detail. These are the weaknesses I am trying to improve using this strategy. The reduction of stress will be greatly appreciated by my family members who oftentimes bear the brunt of my stress. The attention to detail will be appreciated by my colleagues because it will eliminate unnecessary fire drills which easily could have been avoided in our organization, and will allow us to focus on high-level problems and solutions.

What do I do?

- *Is this a plan that is sustainable in the long term? Will accomplishing my short-term wins motivate me to stay on track with my long-term plan?*

  This is a plan that is very manageable on a daily and weekly basis, and will result in some short-term wins early on. The energy from these victories will fuel wins in other areas of my life as well. All of these accomplishments work toward the long-term plan for my life's vision.

What do we believe?

- *Which wins will encourage others to engage in their own personal/professional growth initiatives?*

  My win in being able to lead multiple projects at the same time and in the same organization will inspire others to action. This inspiration is particularly important in motivating the people that I build into these projects and who will eventually lead them.

How do we do this?

- *Are my wins aligned with the larger organizational objectives?*

  My wins are absolutely aligned with the larger organizational objectives. Firstly, being able to reduce stress on unimportant items and focus it on the important ones is very important to enable our team to focus on high-level problem solving and not on putting out fires. Secondly, being able to manage multiple projects at once is important to expanding the bandwidth of our organization's work without sacrificing the quality or the vision.

Creating Your Development Plan

Now that you have followed plans for Demetrius and Jonathan, it is time to complete your worksheets. Based on your assessment results, if you have not done so already, complete the SWOT analysis in Table 4-1 and answer one to three questions from each section in Table 4-2 for yourself. By internalizing your strengths, as well as opportunities, you can identify the gaps that, when filled, will help you accomplish your vision. Additionally, understanding your weaknesses will help you know what to avoid, what to improve, and what personal feedback to request from people skilled in those areas.

This chapter provided you with the tools and templates to create your development plan, and will help to close the gap between where you are today compared with your vision. The plan will greatly enhance your efforts toward actualizing where you want to be, as well as making a positive impact on the world. Keep in mind that it is easy to create a plan that is too ambitious or complex.

We encourage you to commit to small changes you can complete and then update your plan after you have accomplished your initial goals. The next chapter focuses on selecting the guiding team that will help you implement your plan.

Additional Resources

Books

Path of Least Resistance: Learning to Become the Creative Force in Your Own Life. Robert Fritz.

Action Inquiry: The Secret of Timely and Transforming Leadership. William R. Torbert and Associates.

Crucial Conversations: Tools for Talking when Stakes are High. Kerry Patterson, Joseph Grenny, Ron McMillan, and Al Switzler.

Switch: How to Change Things When Change Is Hard. Chip Heath and Dan Heath.

Fifth Discipline Fieldbook: Strategies and Tools for Building a Learning Organization. Art Kleiner, Peter Senge, Richard Ross, Bryan Smith, Charlotte Roberts.

The Life We Were Given: A Long Term Program for Realizing Potential of Body, Mind, Heart and Soul. George Leonard and Michael Murphy.

Polarity Management: Identifying and Managing Unsolvable Problems. Barry Johnson.

DVDs

Integral Life Practice Starter Kit. Integral Institute (3-2-1 shadow workshop and Big Mind).

All Quadrants All Levels Framework (AQAL). Ken Wilber, M.A.

CD

Mindfulness in Motion – A Daily Low Dose Mindfulness Practice. Maryanna Klatt, Ph.D.

Online resource and tools

HeartMath™ meditation practices and emWave to monitor heart activity. www.heartmath.org

Integral Transformative Practice. www.itp-international.org

What do I think/believe?

What do I do?

What do we believe?

How do we do this?

TABLE 5-2: SKILL/BEHAVIOR DEVELOPMENT WORKSHEET
Evaluate and Select Skill/Behavioral Change Priorities – Worksheet

Key Actions	Detailed Action Planning	Behavior 2
Select behaviors	Which behaviors do I want to improve or change? Which behaviors do I perform well that I would like to enhance?	
What are the consequences of this behavior?	What will happen if I continue to demonstrate this behavior in the future? How will my service recipients be impacted? How will my career be impacted? How will my colleagues be impacted? How will my organization be impacted?	
Why do I demonstrate this behavior?	I have developed behaviors over the course of my life because they made sense. What has changed to make this behavior ineffective now?	
How would I like to perform in the future?	Write an end-result statement describing the changes I will make and the impact of those changes. What will an observer see when I have made these changes?	
Who will help me change?	Who could I ask to provide me with feedback on how I am doing? Who could be a good mentor?	
What type of support do I want?	Make an agreement with a person you trust about how you would like to support one another in changing behaviors. How will that person hold me accountable for taking this step? How will I support them in changing their behavior? Is there a group that will support me in the long term?	
What will I do or not do?	What other actions could I take? What am I willing to commit to doing? What am I committed to stopping?	
When will I complete actions?	When will I have completed action items?	

TABLE 5-2: SKILL/BEHAVIOR DEVELOPMENT WORKSHEET
Evaluate and Select Skill/Behavioral Change Priorities – Worksheet

Key Actions	Detailed Action Planning	Behavior 3
Select behaviors	Which behaviors do I want to improve or change? Which behaviors do I perform well that I would like to enhance?	
What are the consequences of this behavior?	What will happen if I continue to demonstrate this behavior in the future? How will my service recipients be impacted? How will my career be impacted? How will my colleagues be impacted? How will my organization be impacted?	
Why do I demonstrate this behavior?	I have developed behaviors over the course of my life because they made sense. What has changed to make this behavior ineffective now?	
How would I like to perform in the future?	Write an end-result statement describing the changes I will make and the impact of those changes. What will an observer see when I have made these changes?	
Who will help me change?	Who could I ask to provide me with feedback on how I am doing? Who could be a good mentor?	
What type of support do I want?	Make an agreement with a person you trust about how you would like to support one another in changing behaviors. How will that person hold me accountable for taking this step? How will I support them in changing their behavior? Is there a group that will support me in the long term?	
What will I do or not do?	What other actions could I take? What am I willing to commit to doing? What am I committed to stopping?	
When will I complete actions?	When will I have completed action items?	

CHAPTER 6
Step 4: Build Your Team and Communicate

In this chapter, you will begin to identify the individuals you want to support your personal and professional development, and the specific roles you envision them playing during this transition. After selecting these people, you will consider the best ways to communicate your needs and receive their feedback. Here, you will carefully choose individuals you feel will be most supportive of your growth. Consider who is involved in your development and who is not. Your selection criteria should include: experience and skills in areas you want to develop, level of unconditional personal support, ability to offer constructive and valuable feedback, capacity to support your transformation, and ability to offer professional support and advocacy.

You will benefit from choosing a diverse yet trusted set of people to support your development. This is particularly beneficial if you plan to make changes that will significantly impact them as well. These people can come from various areas of your life, both personal and professional, and can have differing levels of involvement. Some, for example, could be fairly casual, such as a co-worker who is willing to give you feedback after a meeting about a specific behavior you may be experimenting with to meet a goal about improved interpersonal skills. At the other end of the spectrum, you could engage in a more methodical, long-term agreement with a formal mentor or coach. You will also want to consider the role your spouse or partner plays if you are involved in a relationship. Anyone involved must agree to give you honest and supportive feedback. The common thread for the people you ultimately invite to share in your journey is a firm trust and belief that, above all else, their support is unquestionably in the interest and service of your growth and success.

As another option, your development support could be found within a team setting. For example, if your goal is to run a marathon, your development support could come from a range of sources. It could be as simple as joining a running group to support a fitness goal. You might recruit very specific individual running partners. Other options could include finding expertise from third-party sources like running magazines or online groups that discuss tips and progress. You may even select a group where the explicit purpose is to strongly hold each other more accountable.

Professional development can be supported in similar ways. You have a broad range of choices when looking for support. Organizations range from coaching and training firms to companies that help you improve your presentation skills. Depending on your needs, your individual selection of development support may have components of some or all of these choices. Some may be focused on hard skills, while others, like a coach, generally take on a more supportive role.

After you have selected your support team, the next step will be deciding on methods for each person to communicate authentic feedback. This is the stage where you ask others for specific kinds of support, including possible behavioral changes on their part. You will be letting people around you know that you are engaged in a process of ambitious personal growth and that you want their feedback. Because people often create a sense of personal safety by being able to predict how others around them behave, it is important to inform the people closest to you that you are taking on a structured change process that may involve behaviors with which they are likely to be unfamiliar. The key message here should convey that this process will take time and you will use these new behaviors with varying levels of effectiveness until you master them. You may say you are changing and yet act inconsistently for some period of time while you master new skills.

While the information you share will change over time, the need for communication is critical throughout your development process. Communication will happen with different groups of people at various times, and will likely take on different tones depending on the audience and degree of impact. Some people will simply need to understand that overall change is underway. You will want others to make significant contributions to support your behavioral change. What you communicate and when will depend on your relationship with the individual or group, and the type of support you are asking for.

During your process, you may also be asking others to change. For example, in the workplace you may be communicating information beyond just the scope of work in order to help your staff, coworkers, associates, employees, and direct reports develop stronger business acumen. Moreover, you may want others to change their overall style of communication with you. As you model these new behaviors, be aware that some of your colleagues will adapt quite naturally, while others will require more specific and formal discussions to adjust to this new way of relating. As another example, you may want to delegate more and possibly different tasks, as well as give people more freedom to determine how they accomplish assigned tasks. In this case, you could open a dialogue explaining that you are trusting them to determine the most effective approach and will be available to offer support if additional input is needed. Though many employees would respond favorably to the openness, some will likely be confused if you are not explicit with what you are trying to accomplish.

Support Team Selection Criteria

Providing support to someone who is committed to a process of personal growth is an honor and a tremendous responsibility. It is important to select a support team judiciously since you are asking these individuals to be trusted advisors.

The following is a rough list of key selection factors as a starting point for you to consider when selecting your team. You may find other factors that are also important to you.

Performance: Consider selecting people who have mastered concepts, skills, or behaviors that you would like to develop in yourself. Performance could be as simple as that person having expertise in your field, or a field you want to explore. He could have strong interpersonal skills and empathy, or have hard skills such as financial analysis that you would like to enhance in yourself. These individuals could also be people you respect in general. If you are focused on developing advanced leadership skills, you could certainly benefit from the mentoring and support of someone you believe is successful against these measures.

Coaching: Consider having a person who is paid as an independent expert in the process of development or therapy. Most have undergone rigorous training or have significant experience in the field to support your development and success. As they are independent, they are generally free of the natural bias held by family members, friends, and colleagues. Working with the right coach can be very valuable, significantly accelerate the development process, and help you overcome barriers.

Therapy: Having someone who is an experienced psychotherapist can be very beneficial. A good therapist who is a good fit with your style and needs can help you make changes much more quickly and efficiently than if you try to work through issues yourself.

Personal or Family Connection: People from your family supporting your development could include siblings, a partner or a spouse, or a close friend who feels like family. Ideally, they will help you maintain a balanced perspective of your life as a whole based on a historical connection, rather than just the immediate view of a new coach or therapist. They will also help you think through the impact of your changes on your family system. It is important to balance your development and professional focus with your family commitments.

Willingness and ability to commit time to your development: This is imperative. Ask those committed to supporting your development how to optimize your time together, and also discuss your mutual needs. The idea is that everyone should benefit from a clear understanding of how to both support the growth process and create healthy reciprocity. It will also be important to consider the time commitment you desire. Be willing to explore options that allow you to minimize the amount of time you request. You may consider creative options like volunteering for a board that your mentor or support person is on. This would allow you to learn directly and also support that person in meeting their objectives.

It is important to know not only who to select, but also who to avoid. Keep in mind that there are many very well-meaning people who would love to help, but, realistically, who are overcommitted and cannot provide the type of support you seek. Others may lack strong support skills, such as the ability to give open and honest feedback. If someone lacks the time or skills to provide helpful advice delivered in a supportive way, you should not include them. What you do not need during an intense development process is to waste time and energy with someone whose involvement could derail you.

Tools

The following worksheets are designed to help you connect your development action plan with the people who will help you accomplish these goals. They will fulfill different roles, ranging from encouragement and support to providing skilled expertise. You might also choose to include those who may be more directly impacted by the changes you are making. The more information you can provide during the process, the more likely they will be to support you or communicate their concerns to help you accomplish your goals. For an example, see Demetrius and Jonathan's answers following each worksheet.

TABLE 6-1: SUPPORT TEAM WORKSHEET Support Team Worksheet				
Goal	**Type of Support I Need**	**Role**	**Skills/ Knowledge**	**Arrangement**

Development Journey Continued

When we last connected with Demetrius and Jonathan, they had each created development plans. They are now evaluating who will help them implement their goals.

SUPPORT TEAM WORKSHEET – DEMETRIUS'S EXAMPLE

Goal	Type of Support I Need	Role	Skills/Knowledge	Arrangement
Enhance verbal communication skills	Speaking Coach	◾ Gives me exercises and practices ◾ Provides feedback on behavioral experiments ◾ Open to practicing new behaviors	Toastmaster (Gold Level) Comfortable with pointing out Communication errors and how to correct those errors	Participation in the local Toastmaster's club
Become physically healthier	Healthy friends	◾ Engage in and reinforce healthy behaviors ◾ Provide feedback on behavioral experiments ◾ Open to practicing new behaviors	Workout regimens ◾ running ◾ aerobics ◾ weights	Mutual support
Start a business	Mentor, entrepreneur	◾ Provide network connections ◾ Discuss strategy	History as an entrepreneur	Weekly conversations

SUPPORT TEAM WORKSHEET – JONATHAN'S EXAMPLE

Goal	Type of Support I Need	Role	Skills/Knowledge	Arrangement
Able to let go of insignificant things, and take action on the details that do matter	Family members and my personal /professional mentor	◾ Helps me to keep perspective and prioritize things ◾ Keeps me accountable for personal and logistical management	Experience working in complex situations Experience in having both a career and a personal life/family at the same time, and managing both well	Bi-weekly calls or in-person meetings with my mentors Weekly communication with my parents and two brothers
Able to identify multiple opportunities, create multiple projects, and build multiple teams within the same organization at the same time	Professional mentor	Coaches me on organizing and prioritizing feelings / thoughts/ ideas, and then creating an action plan around more than one at the same time; these action plans synchronize larger organizational objectives	Experience working in complex situations Experience serving in multiple roles at the same time within the same organization	Bi-weekly calls or in-person meetings with my mentor

Once you determine your support team and their corresponding roles, you will want to figure out communication, timing, and expectations. This is the place to consider the kind of feedback you might expect from others to ensure you are making meaningful progress. This communication can provide you with invaluable information and feedback that is critical for your success. Since your plan is based on your own intuitive senses, the ongoing data should confirm your assumptions and serve as a feedback mechanism to refine your thinking.

TABLE 6-2: COMMUNICATION PLAN WORKSHEET
Communication Planning Worksheet

Who	What to Communicate	What They Can Expect From You	What You Want From Them	How Often

The following are Communication Worksheets from Demetrius and Jonathan. You can use them as examples of how one may use communication when managing change both personally and within an organization.

COMMUNICATION PLANNING WORKSHEET – DEMETRIUS'S EXAMPLE				
Who	**What to Communicate**	**What They Can Expect From You**	**What You Want From Them**	**How Often**
Wife	How am I doing against my major goals? How are my changes impacting you? Us? Practice inquiry skills	As I become more centered, my reactions to difficult issues will be more thoughtful As I learn to take more perspectives, I will offer additional insights and also ask questions to better understand his perspective Additional questions about how my "behavioral experiments" are doing	Listening Feedback Recommendations Understanding	Check in daily
Leadership Team	How am I doing against my major goals? How are my changes impacting you? Us? Practice inquiry skills Share reflections and ask for their reflections	As I become more centered, my reactions to difficult issues will be more thoughtful As I learn to take more perspectives, I will offer additional insights and also ask questions to better understand their perspectives Grow the organization in ways we jointly define and refine Additional questions about how my "behavioral experiments" are doing Discussions that contain additional reflections to provide more context for decision making	Listening Feedback Recommendations	Check in weekly
Friends	I am making some personal changes and I would like feedback as I try new behaviors	Additional questions about how my "behavioral experiments" are doing Discussions that contain additional reflections to provide more contexts for decision making	Feedback Recommendations	Ad hoc

COMMUNICATION PLANNING WORKSHEET – JONATHAN'S EXAMPLE

Who	What to Communicate	What They Can Expect From You	What You Want From Them	How Often
Family members (parents and brothers)	How well am I managing my personal life (i.e., health, finances, home, plan of personal improvement, etc.)? How true am I remaining to my overarching vision and values?	I am continually improving my ability to manage the small details in life that are important, and to let go of the ones that are not. I am continually prioritizing the tasks and responsibilities I face, both personally and professionally. I am accomplishing my vision in the framework of my values	Time to discuss my areas of progress and needed improvement. Proactive accountability in the areas in which I am weak. Encouragement to let go of insignificant items and to focus my attention on the important ones	Weekly calls
Personal and professional mentors	How well am I managing my professional life (i.e., education, work experience, plan for professional improvement, etc.)? How well am I prioritizing and managing multiple projects at the same time, and what are the results? How true am I remaining to my overarching vision and values?	I am continually prioritizing the tasks and responsibilities I face, both personally and professionally. I am prioritizing and managing multiple projects at the same time which are delivering substantial impact collectively toward organizational goals. I am accomplishing my vision in the framework of my values.	Time to discuss my areas of progress and needed development. Experience in managing complex situations and multiple projects at once within the same organization	Bi-weekly calls/ meetings
Business partners	How am I doing in prioritizing and managing each of the projects for which I am responsible? How well do these projects align in progressing toward accomplishing our shared vision, in the framework of our shared values?	Deliver excellent results for each of my projects which cumulatively create progress toward our organizational goals. The same type of information that I am seeking from them, about their projects. Feedback on their progress. Unwavering commitment to accomplishing our shared vision in the framework of our shared values	Time to discuss my areas of progress and needed development. Time, resources, and flexibility to experiment and execute my projects in creative and unconventional ways	Daily meetings and correspondence

Innovative Leadership Reflection Questions

To help you develop your action plan, it is time to further clarify your direction using reflection questions. The questions for "What do I think/believe?" reflect your intentions. "What do I do?" questions reflect your actions. The questions "What do we believe?" reflect the culture of your organization (i.e., work, school, community), and "How do we do this?" questions reflect systems and processes for your organization. This exercise is an opportunity to practice innovative leadership by considering your vision for yourself and how it will play out in the context of your life. You will define your intentions, actions, culture, and systems in a systematic manner.

Table 6-3 contains an exhaustive list of questions to appeal to a broad range of readers. A few will likely fit your own personal situation; focus on the ones that seem the most relevant. We recommend you answer one to three questions from each of the categories.

TABLE 6-3: QUESTIONS TO GUIDE THE LEADER AND ORGANIZATION

What do I think/believe?

- What qualities do I want in the people I ask to support my personal change?
- What qualities will I eliminate from my current and future team?
- How do I think my change will impact those close to me?
- Will my change help those close to me become more successful according to their definition of success?
- Why would others spend their time and energy to help me develop?
- How much support do I expect from others?
- Am I making reasonable requests of those close to me?
- Am I looking for others in the social service arena who are making similar changes?
- Do I want people around me to change along with me?
- Do I need to improve my communication skills to improve my ability to seek support for my growth? Do I understand that my effectiveness in communicating to others as well as listening to their feedback hinges on my ability to communicate effectively?
- Because my development may be a very personal and even private choice, what am I willing to communicate to others?
- How do I think my preference for privacy or sharing will impact others'?
- What personal stories (actions and emotions) will convey my commitment to my personal change in a heartfelt manner while also empowering others to act?
- Do I need to communicate anything to the organization or just to my support group?

What do I do?

- Who do I ask to participate in my change?

- How do I determine and communicate the criteria for the right people to support me? "Right" includes personality traits, innate capabilities, skills, knowledge, time, and willingness

- Once I know the criteria, who are the right people and how do I figure out which roles I would like them to take to support my success? How do I invite them to support this important personal transformation?

- Who do I need to support my development for it to be successful? How can my personal development activities or successes help these key people meet their personal objectives?

- Who may become a barrier to my change? How do I mitigate their negative impact? What are immediate steps and longer-term actions?

- What commitments and actions should I take that demonstrate my belief that change is possible?

- How do I "walk the talk" and show my conviction through my actions? Am I making the changes I say I will? Am I making the changes I say I will?

- How do I ask for feedback? Am I clear about what information would be helpful to me and what information would not be helpful?

- How do I convey my request for input and support when I fall short of my stated goals at points along the way?

- How do I deliver messages tailored to different supporters that motivate them to continue to help me accomplish my goals?

- Can I be a role model for others during my change process to encourage them to expand their own capabilities?

- How do I demonstrate humility and genuinely appreciate the support others are providing?

- How do I communicate that the balance between challenge and overload is important, and that I want to maintain balance as I move toward meeting my personal vision?

- How do I communicate my need and desire for accurate feedback?

- What do I communicate when my situation and priorities change?

What do we believe?

- What are the social and cultural norms that dictate the type of support I should ask for and expect?

- How do we use my personal change as an opportunity to test new behaviors and demonstrate their positive impact on the group (professional organization, family, community)?

- Do the current social and cultural norms still fit for where I am/we are going?

- Do I have the right support to change the culture of our group to allow me to sustain the changes I am trying to make?

- What are our beliefs about who does the communicating? How much information do they share? How often? Do we solicit input or just convey information?

- What is the appropriate language and message for each audience segment (organization, family, community)?

- What type of feedback will I seek from others to determine if they are supportive of my personal changes?

- Does our current organizational culture and approach to communicating support me in making the changes I am trying to make?

> **How do we do this?**
>
> - What are the key skills and behaviors that support my transformation and are necessary to my team? What are the gaps between my current support team and the team needed to support transformation?
>
> - Do I have the right people available with the right skills and behaviors? Do I need to augment my support team with professionals such as a coach, therapist, spiritual advisor, clergy, colleague, or boss?
>
> - What is the best combination of approaches for me to meet my support needs? Does this include hiring a coach or scheduling regular lunches with a trusted colleague?
>
> - What trust-building activities can we conduct to improve my degree of comfort with those supporting me?
>
> - What personal and professional metrics should I track to understand if I am seeking and receiving the appropriate level of support?
>
> - If the transformation is a long one, how do I acknowledge the support others are providing? What happens if someone I thought would be a good supporter does not work out, such as a colleague changing jobs or moving out of the area?
>
> - Am I communicating what supporters believe is important to them? Do they see the progress they hope to see?
>
> - How do I communicate wins to stakeholders to sustain their reinforcement and energy?
>
> - What is my communication approach and plan? Who wants information? When? Through what medium? What are the key messages? How do I keep multiple supporters informed with the right amount of information at the right time to enhance buy-in and support for my behavioral change?

Demetrius's Responses to Reflection Questions

We will now walk through Demetrius's answers to one or two questions from each section of Table 6-3. Simply follow along with Demetrius to answer the questions for yourself, or select the questions that fit your current situation.

What do I think/believe?

- *What qualities do I want in the people I ask to support my personal change?*

  I want the people I ask to support my personal change to be open and honest without fear of hurting my feelings. I believe in order for me to successfully change in the areas I have identified, it's crucial for people to feel they can be honest. There have been times in my life that I didn't necessarily like the feedback I was given, nonetheless I recognized the feedback helped in my overall growth. For that reason, I value open feedback.

- *How do I think my change will impact those closest to me?*

  I look at this from a couple of perspectives. With regard to my wife, I believe this change will help us to grow closer as a unit because I will be investing time and energy in learning to be more open in communicating. Since she will be part of my leadership change team, she will have the opportunity to give me open feedback on how my changes are affecting her, and us, at all levels.

From a corporate standpoint, I hope this change strengthens the healthy communication we currently share on my different teams. Throughout my MBA program I have conducted a multitude of leadership experiments with my team, and they have been more than willing to indulge me in these experiments. I hope that as they walk with me on this journey helping me to grow, they experience growth within themselves as well.

- *How much support do I expect from others?*

I expect to receive a great deal of support from the individuals I would like to walk with me on this journey. They have all shown me tremendous support in the past. Without them I would not be the person I am today, and I certainly would not be where I am today.

What do I do?

- *Who do I want to ask to participate in my change?*

I have asked my wife to be a primary development partner because she knows me better than anyone else and has always been one of my biggest supporters. She will be the most affected by many of the changes I make. I'm also hoping that as I make changes, she finds an avenue to make the personal changes she desires for herself. I will also ask a valued colleague and executive within my firm whom I trust to give me sound advice and invaluable feedback. He is at a stage in his career now where I would like to be in the future. Because we will approach the end result from different perspectives, getting his opinion will only make the experience better.

- *How do I convey my request for input and support when I fall short of my stated goals at points along the way?*

I believe that falling short would be a great opportunity for reflection and understanding, and I would talk with my development team to understand why I fell short and to devise a way to ensure I don't do it again. One thing I have learned in my career as a project manager is that it's important to readily admit when there is an issue to be addressed, determine viable solutions, and construct a mechanism for how to minimize the likelihood of repeating the behaviors that led to the issue in the first place. This is the same approach I would take to minimize the likelihood of falling short of my goals again.

What do we believe?

- *Do I have the right support to change the culture of our group to allow me to sustain the changes I am trying to make?*

I believe I do. The individuals I have selected are receptive to change when the change is moving the culture in a positive direction that is in line with the overall goals of the group they represent. For my wife it's a matter of whether the goals help us to grow as a family in a manner that will sustain us in the future. For my organization it's about adding value to both the organization and to the clients that we work with. For my friends it's a question of how we stay close and continue to grow our friendships as we all embark on divergent journeys.

■ *What are our beliefs about communication with regard to who does the communicating? How much information do they share? How often? Do we solicit input or just convey information?*

Soliciting input is quite important to let me know how I am being received and how I can improve. I continue to seek a great deal of feedback to understand how much information people want from me, how often, and in what format. I believe the part of communication that I fail on most often is simply listening, digesting, and then responding to the communication I have received. I believe if I solicit more and convey information that is expected from me, then, my overall communication efforts will improve.

How do we do this?

■ *How do I communicate wins to stakeholders to sustain their reinforcement and energy?*

I approach this differently than one would expect. I don't communicate wins to the stakeholders, they communicate wins to me. Part of my job as a project manager is to ensure the delivery of a product at the agreed upon time and the agreed upon price—preferably we exceed both goals. Part of the approach is to review the product with the stakeholders on a biweekly basis so they can see how it's functioning and to allow for course corrections if necessary. My win comes when I hear them say, "This is exactly what we were looking for. We can't wait to see what you have for us next. If you need anything more from us, let us know so we don't impede your progress." When I hear comments like this, I know we are going down the right path and I know the stakeholders are fully invested and are communicating well.

Jonathan's Responses to Reflection Questions

We will now walk through Jonathan's answers to one or two questions from each section of Table 6-3.

What do I think/ believe?

■ *What qualities do I want in the people I ask to support my personal change?*

Within my family, I can call upon my parents and either of my brothers to provide me with the support I need to make this personal change. They all know me extremely well on a personal level and are supportive of my desire for personal improvement. With personal and professional mentors, I engage a wide variety of people, but, to make the specific changes which I have listed there are a couple of qualities that I consider to be critical. One is that my mentors need to have practical experience in the areas in which I am working and in which I plan to work. I highly value the advice of people who have "been there and done that," and who are tactically competent and emotionally intelligent in my specific field. Another important quality for a mentor is a commitment to truly help me make these personal changes. This commitment may require spending significant time outside of a normal routine to keep me accountable and make recommendations needed for my personal development. Finally, a mentor should be someone who shares similar personal values to mine. I take much more seriously the advice from a person who is operating in the same framework of values as I am; it also makes communication and understanding much easier.

What do I do?

■ *How do I communicate that the balance between challenge and overload is important, and that I want to maintain balance as I move toward meeting my personal vision?*

I choose mentors who understand how busy I am, and, thus, they help me to realistically prioritize and plan personal development in a way that is consistent with my schedule. It is important that during a mentoring session, the first thing I do is update my mentor on everything going on in my life. This way, my mentor is reminded of how many balls I am juggling, and keeps advice focused and relevant to my current situation. My time with mentors also allows me an hour or two to step away from the daily grind and look at things on a higher level, which is often hard to do in the workplace.

What do we believe?

■ *Does our current organizational culture and approach to communicating support me in making the changes I am trying to make?*

Because we founded our own organization, we were fortunate enough to instill a lot of the organizational values from day one. As young founders with so little experience at the time, we made learning and self-improvement key values—and these have really defined a lot of the culture and accomplishments of our organization. I personally encouraged my colleagues to pursue the topics and items of personal development which intrigued them, and I did the same. As a result, we all were able to find our respective niche and become experts in that area. This developed expertise has helped us to be very good at what we do as an organization. This culture prevails, and makes personal change something very ordinary, yet held in high regard in our organization.

How do we do this?

- *What trust-building activities can we conduct to improve my degree of comfort with those supporting me?*

  To me, the most important trust-building activity is for my mentor and I to be straightforward and honest with each other in all things. If that is not the case, then true mentoring and self-improvement will not happen. I view my mentor as someone with whom I can be incredibly open and in whom I can place a lot of trust—and it actually is quite a relief to be able to confide in someone about the things which are not typically discussed in the workplace or in family settings.

Build Your Team and Communicate

Now that you have seen the worksheets and read through the sample case narratives, it is time to complete the worksheets and answer the questions for yourself if you have not done so already. We encourage you to complete all of the exercises. Based on your support preferences, complete Table 6-1 (Support Team worksheet) and Table 6-2 (Communication Planning worksheet), then answer one to three questions from each section in Table 6-3.

This chapter serves to help you clarify your supporters and communication plan as you begin defining your feedback sources. This is the plan that will provide you with expertise, emotional support, buy-in, and feedback for your development. While creating a communication plan may seem extraneous, never underestimate the value of both emotional and moral support, and communication to and from those who will be affected by your changes. This could be as simple as talking to your spouse or family about the way your changing routine may impact them, while letting them know you appreciate their willingness to be flexible.

Resources

Book:
Crucial Conversations: Tools for Talking when Stakes are High. Patterson, Grenny, McMillan, Switzler.

Fifth Discipline Fieldbook: Strategies and Tools for Building a Learning Organization. Kleiner, Senge, Ross, Smith, Roberts.

What do I think/believe?

What do I do?

What do we believe?

How do we do this?

CHAPTER 7
Step 5: Take Action

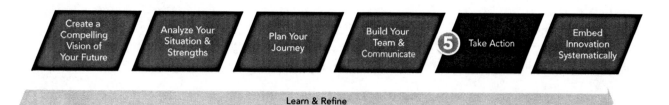

Create a Compelling Vision of Your Future → Analyze Your Situation & Strengths → Plan Your Journey → Build Your Team & Communicate → ⑤ Take Action → Embed Innovation Systematically

Learn & Refine

Now that you have created a plan to become an innovative leader and have defined your support team, it is time to take action. Your plan should spell out which actions you want to take, how often, and who can support your progress.

As you begin realizing your vision, you may start to identify challenges to your growth and development. Barriers are simply a normal part of any transformative process, and we have provided a number of useful tools to help pinpoint and navigate them successfully.

An important part of your success is believing that you can make progress and sustain growth in your leadership ability. You developed a strong foundation by creating a compelling vision and analyzing unique challenges and opportunities to determine what actions you need to take to achieve your goals.

Be aware that this stage can take tremendous focus and energy. Many people stumble here, especially when the change process becomes difficult and the demands of balancing life requirements take on greater urgency. Think, for example, of how many times you may have joined a gym, but did not follow your plan to go there as frequently as you'd intended. Implementing your plan requires a deep commitment to your growth and also an understanding of the barriers you will face based on your personality type or history with implementing change. As barriers surface, you have the ability to remove them or modify your course with the support of your team.

With this in mind, allow yourself some flexibility in your development process instead of viewing your plan as fixed. See your plan as an initial starting point, or a working hypothesis about how you will develop. With that perspective, you can better use the challenges you face as a way to provide feedback on your original hypothesis and modify it as you go along. In other words, rather than viewing these obstacles as threats, you have the opportunity to naturally incorporate them as fine-tuning mechanisms. For each challenge you face, carefully consider the unique learning opportunity and how to use it to help you implement your plan. Since personal development is a long-term journey, you will have many opportunities to face these challenges and take corrective actions.

Lastly, your support team will play a crucial role in helping make the plan sustainable. They will offer you input and feedback as well as encouragement during times when you struggle. Even though you specifically chose the changes and goals within your plan, it is often still helpful to have a built-in system of accountability. When you run into inner resistance and difficulty, connect with someone who will remind you that you are already competent and that you can meet these goals in the same way you have met many other challenges.

Tools

The following worksheet helps you to anticipate barriers and mitigate them while implementing your action plan. You can refer to the completed case sample worksheets as examples.

TABLE 7-1: BARRIERS ACTION PLANNING WORKSHEET

Category	Barrier	Impact of Barrier	How to Remove or Work Around	Support I Need to Remove or Work Around
In my thinking				
In my behavior				
In our beliefs				
In how we do things				

Demetrius's Development Journey Continued

When we last met Demetrius, he was building his support team and defining how he wanted to communicate.

	BARRIER ACTION PLANNING WORKSHEET – DEMETRIUS'S EXAMPLE			
Category	Barrier	Impact of Barrier	How to Remove or Work Around	Support I Need to Remove or Work Around
In my thinking	I think my family and friends expect perfection in everything I do—failure is not an option	I may not challenge myself as much as I could to ensure I don't fail	Use the advice of trusted mentors and challenge myself more without the fear of failure because even in failure there is a learning experience	Ask my family and friends to believe in my approach and not constantly worry about failure
In my behavior	I analyze all possible outcomes before making any decisions	Sometimes I take too long to make a decision; thus, miss out on the opportunity	Trust my gut feeling more often and be prepared to move forward	Ask my support team to hold me accountable to trusting my gut feeling more often
In our beliefs	We believe everyone within the firm is interested in career growth	We ignore the individuals who are happy within their current career believing they are lazy in their work	Recognize those who are happy where they are and applaud their contributions as much as those who are looking to grow	We should not force career growth on others because it may alienate them and be the impetus to move to another firm that values their worth just as they are
In how we do things	People expect things to stay the same when change is necessary	Friction among detractors to change	Continue to shine the light on why change is necessary and the positive aspects of change	Continue to share goals with everyone who is affected

Jonathan's Development Journey Continued

When we last met Jonathan, he was building his support team and defining how he wanted to communicate

BARRIER ACTION PLANNING WORKSHEET – JONATHAN'S EXAMPLE

Category	Barrier	Impact of Barrier	How to Remove or Work Around	Support I Need to Remove or Work Around
In my thinking	I want this to be high quality, so I will think about it now and execute later when I have full energy and resources	This delay sometimes causes me to miss opportunities	Adapting and prioritizing my thinking and actions Accepting that not everything needs to be perfect to be successful – sometimes taking it part of the way and passing it to others is my job	Personal/professional mentorship in prioritizing and managing in complex and resource-limited situations
In my behavior	I like to work on a lot of different things at the same time to keep it interesting	Sometimes I take too long to make a decision; thus, miss out on the opportunity	This constant shift in focus causes me to operate in crisis-management mode and wait until the last minute to finish things	Personal/professional mentorship in prioritizing and managing in complex and resource-limited settings
In our beliefs	We over-analyze our actions before we take them	This can cause us to find so many issues with a potential action that we choose not to take it and lose the opportunity it presented	Deciding things with more faith in our own skill and resources Operating with a higher risk tolerance Improving our resilience to failure when it occurs	As a team, keep each other accountable to not be overly practical and analytical As a team, pushing each other to take risk when necessary to get something done
In how we do things	We try to do everything that is put before us by others, in order to take advantage of opportunities and build good will	This gives people outside of our organization control of where we are spending our time and effort	We need to say "no" more often We need to delegate tasks that pull us away from primary responsibilities to non-management staff within our organization. This means identifying what to delegate and training others to handle the tasks	As a team, keeping each other accountable to our vision statement and encouraging partners to stay on task and say "no" when necessary

Innovative Leadership Reflection Questions

To help you develop your action plan, it is time to further clarify your direction using reflection questions. The questions for "What do I think/believe?" reflect your intentions. "What do I do?" questions reflect your actions. The questions "What do we believe?" reflect the culture of your organization (i.e., work, school, community), and "How do we do this?" questions reflect systems and processes for your organization. This exercise is an opportunity to practice innovative leadership by considering your vision for yourself and how it will play out in the context of your life. You will define your intentions, actions, culture, and systems in a systematic manner.

Table 7-2 contains a thorough list of questions to appeal to a broad range of readers. You will likely find some that best fit your own personal situation; focus on those that seem the most relevant. We recommend you answer one to three questions from each of the categories.

TABLE 7-2: QUESTIONS TO GUIDE THE LEADER AND ORGANIZATION

What do I think/believe?

- In what ways do I need to change my perspective or skills to succeed?
- To become more effective, what do I need to change about how I see myself or the world?
- Including beliefs, what do I need to let go of to make these changes?
- What do I see as my individual role? How does this role allow me to fit in different organizations, including my family?
- How can I effectively grow and empower myself? How do I support my success as well as the success of the organization(s)?
- How can I benefit from my own personal growth and development?

What do I do?

- What feedback do I seek that will allow me to correct, redirect, or recalibrate my behavior and feel motivated to make necessary changes?
- How do I request clear and concise feedback that allows me to grow and supports the growth of others?
- How do I determine what I am ready to change within myself and what additional support I require for those changes I am resisting?
- What help am I willing to request? Am I investing appropriate time and/or money to support my growth? Is the commitment I am making to my personal change consistent with the results I expect to receive?
- What creative solutions can I find to increase my personal awareness? Do I track my performance against my goals using logs or reflection activities?
- How will I identify times when my own behavior undermines my success? What will I do when I find my own behavior undermines my success?
- Can I treat my own differing commitments as learning opportunities?
- How do I encourage "bad news" as well as good from my support team?
- Am I looking for opportunities to visibly demonstrate my progress as my development process unfolds?
- What am I doing to retain my support team as time goes on?
- How do I manage my transformation over time? How do I focus on accomplishing my daily tasks while concurrently focusing sufficient time on my vision and goals?

What do we believe?

- How will my changes impact my ability to be successful, based on the organization's reward system, and given its values, goals, and culture?

- What are the stories within the organization about effective leadership? How do my personal changes position me going forward?

- How can we connect prior leadership development successes to my current development effort? How can we use prior success to reinforce our ability to navigate current leadership changes?

- What parts of our past failures were attributed to leadership? Do my development changes appear positive to the organization's success or are they threatening?

- Does our culture support the behavioral traits I am trying to develop?

How do we do this?

- What processes do we have that may serve as barriers to my developing in the way I would like? Am I in a position to change the systems to remove these barriers? If so, how involved and complex will those changes be? If I cannot remove the barriers, how will I navigate around them?

- Are my changes aligned with the organization's guiding principles? If not, how do I navigate the gaps between them?

- Do the organizational structure and governance approach support my personal development? If not, what options do I have to resolve barriers to my growth?

- What early warning metrics can I track to let me know what impact my behavioral changes have on others? What leading indicators will alert me before any significant issues arise?

- How can I leverage current or generally accepted mastery frameworks to gain support of others and explain the changes I am trying to make?

- How do my changes fit into the current organizational reward system? If there are misalignments, what will I do to navigate the barriers and challenges?

- Have I clearly articulated the changes I want to make and asked for the support of those around me?

- What communication processes do we use to provide timely feedback? How will these impact me during my development? How will my development impact others?

- What is the organization doing to measure, communicate, and fund my development and activities?

Demetrius's Responses to Reflection Questions

We will now walk through Demetrius's answers to one or two questions from each section of Table 7-2.

What do I think/believe?

- *In what ways do I need to change my perspective or skills to succeed?*

  As I advance toward growth in my career and begin taking steps toward running my own company, I need to look more closely at the bigger picture as opposed to my individual contribution only. I must continue to grow my business acumen to ensure I understand how different components of a business fit together. When I do this, I will have additional value that I can add to the firm.

■ *What do I need to change about myself or the world to be more effective?*

To be more effective, I need to do a better job of articulating an overall plan. Many times I can see a plan clearly in my mind and lead toward that plan. However, I struggle when it comes to expressing aloud the plan with others so that they can implement it. Writing down a plan can help me to verbalize it.

What do I do?

■ *How will I identify when my own behavior undermines my success?*

Self-doubt is the thing that could most undermine my success. The best way to handle this is to recognize when doubt is creeping in and find a way to turn it around. This shift could be to focus on my long-term goals, or to simply remember the commitment I've made to my family. This should help me to dispel self-doubt that could restrict me from moving forward.

■ *How do I encourage "bad news" as well as good from my support team?*

I embrace the bad news as a means of helping me determine which changes I need to make. I know that many people say this, but I actually believe it. Over time, I believe people come to understand this about me, and since I have selected people who already know me well, they understand that I want and can handle the truth when it is delivered compassionately. While most people like to hear the good news, I believe the bad news is what helps drive us to change. I believe it's really hard to grow as a leader if you do not understand how to deal with bad news that may come your way.

What do we believe?

■ *What stories of the past do we need to stop telling because they no longer support our or my success?*

We need to stop telling the stories of our past success and begin to realize and focus on future success. While it's important to never forget the past, it is important not to let the past define the future. Staying stagnant and dwelling in the glory of the past doesn't help current staff, particularly if they weren't there when past successes were celebrated.

■ *Does our culture support the behavioral traits I am trying to develop?*

I believe most companies still focus on the old adage of command and control. The behavior I'm aspiring to is that of leading by guidance. Setting a direction, then allowing your team to achieve a goal by the methods they choose, produces a greater buy-in from all parties involved. This means letting go of the control—and for some people this aspect is scary. While I don't think our culture is there yet, I do see signs of progress toward these traits.

How do we do this?

- *Do the organizational structure and the governance approach support my personal development? If not, what options do I have to remove barriers to my growth?*

  Our firm supports my personal development by encouraging me and other employees to obtain certifications and attend networking events. When the organization offers assistance, feel free to use the support; however, despite what an organization deems important, each of us has to take control of our own destinies in order to fully achieve our personal objectives. As a leader, I believe it's important to look outside of what the organization does to support personal development. I believe it's important to devise your own plan for development and growth.

Jonathan's Responses to Reflection Questions

We will now walk through Jonathan's answers to one or two questions from each section of Table 7-2.

What do I think/believe?

- *Including beliefs, what do I need to let go of to make these changes?*

  I need to let go of some of my notions of success as simply getting things done and making things happen. Success can be partially described as those things, but it should equally be described by how much I develop and grow in doing something. Thus, I need to give myself the flexibility to develop and grow as an equal priority as getting things done, and take more time and energy to improve myself while working.

What do I do?

- *What creative solutions can I find to increase my personal awareness? Do I track my performance against my goals using logs or reflection activities?*

  I do keep several journals in which I sometimes write my thoughts, ideas, and feelings. This is an incredibly effective way to improve my emotional intelligence and clarity of mind. My favorite way to work on my personal awareness, however, is to walk or run in a tranquil place where I can marvel at natural beauty and let my mind wander until it comes back to some firm conclusions and action steps ahead. The more often I do this, the more clearly and directly I can think and act.

How do we do this?

■ *How can I leverage current or generally accepted mastery frameworks to gain support of others and explain the changes I am trying to make?*

There are not time-consuming rubrics and detailed metrics for personal change in our organization. So, it is important that our organization is open to a wide variety of personal and organization improvement activities, and that we rely upon each other's daily feedback to check our progress. We view each other as personal and professional mentors. This development culture has really defined a lot of the success of our organization and makes it a dynamic place to implement personal growth.

Your Process of Taking Action

Now that you have seen the worksheets and read through Demetrius and Jonathan's narratives, it is time to complete the worksheets and answer the questions. We encourage you to complete all of the exercises and answer one to three reflection questions from each section in Table 7-2. This process serves to help you clarify what your barriers to success are, and how you will manage or remove them.

This chapter summarizes the basics for identifying barriers to your ability to successfully accomplish your goals as described in your plan. It also asks you to monitor the systems you put into place to measure your success and take corrective action. The next chapter will walk you through the process of ensuring that the changes you make are sustainable.

Additional Resources

Book

Action Inquiry: The Secret of Timely and Transforming Leadership. William R. Torbert and Associates.

How the Way We Talk can Change the Way We Work: Seven Languages for Transformation. Robert Kegan and Lisa Laskow Lahey.

DVD

Shadow Module 3-2-1 Process with Diane Hamilton. Integral Life Practice Series produced by Integral Institute.

What do I think/believe?

What do I do?

What do we believe?

How do we do this?

CHAPTER 8
Step 6: Embed Innovation Systematically

Congratulations! You have made it to the final chapter in your development process. You are now ready to shift from implementing your plan as something with a discrete end to considering how you will integrate these changes into your lifestyle going forward. We suggest you view your leadership development as an ongoing process rather than something to check off the to-do list. Given the volume of change we are facing now and expect to face in the future, continual development is a must simply to stay current. In this light, you can begin asking yourself, "What supports can I put into place to stay on track? How can I gain additional benefits from ongoing practice?"

To maintain momentum, it is critical to retain a sense of urgency and minimize any complacency that may come from early success. Be aware that it is easy to stray from your goals if you declare success based on your early results, especially when other areas of your life tug at your time and attention. One helpful shift in thinking is to see the actions you are taking as a practice. You are practicing your leadership skills in the same fashion that a professional athlete practices a particular sport. The most successful athletes are constantly working to improve, even though they may already be the best in the world. This is why many of them remain successful over a long period of time. You will need to consider a long-term commitment to activities that foster success and help maintain your momentum.

So, ask yourself, "When I see progress, what will keep me motivated to continue practicing? I need some reminder that my progress is a result of engaged practice, and my performance is likely to suffer if I do not maintain proper focus."

At this point, you may want to re-evaluate your goals and begin raising the bar. You will need to balance long-term practice that sustains progress with identifying your next developmental focus or goals.

Altogether, this step invites you to be more conscious of actions as well as tangible barriers, to identify the elements in your life that support the continual realization of your goals, and examine the events and relationships that interfere with your vision and goals. It is critical to remove as many barriers as possible and to stop behaviors that no longer align with your development goals.

The overall objective in this chapter is to understand your habits and choices, and to confirm they are aligned with your long-term goals.

Tools

Below is a table you can use to capture and track your progress. For many people, the simple act of recording their progress in writing helps maintain their commitment. Use the following worksheet to help track your progress against each of your goals. If you would like to see a sample, review Demetrius and Jonathan's answers later in this chapter.

TABLE 8-1 PERSONAL TRANSFORMATION ACTIVITY/PRACTICE LOG TEMPLATE

Goal	Action	Record Actual Performance	Expected Impact	Priority	Measure	Progress	Feedback from Whom
Top 1	1.						
	2.						
	3.						
Top 2	4.						
	5.						
	6.						
Top 3	7.						
	8.						
	9.						

Demetrius's Development Journey Continued

When we last met Demetrius, he was taking action on his development plan. Demetrius will now walk through his worksheets and journal entries for embedding change systematically.

PERSONAL TRANSFORMATION ACTIVITY/PRACTICE LOG - DEMETRIUS'S EXAMPLE							
Goal	Action	Record Actual Performance	Expected Impact	Priority	Measure	Progress	Feedback From Whom
Top 1	Think before responding to disagreeable information	Mon - yes Tues - yes Wed - no Thurs - no Friday - yes	Refrain from speaking with emotion	1	Frequency of meeting goal	Met goal 3x this week	Spouse – impact of calm Colleague – impact of composure
Top 2	Exercise 30 minutes a day three days a week	Mon - none Tues - 35 Wed - 40 Thurs - 30 Friday - none	Healthier body and mind	1	Frequency of meeting goal	Met goal	Spouse – support for sticking with goal
Top 3	4.						
	5.						
	6.						
Top 4	7.						
	8.						
	9.						

Jonathan's Development Journey Continued

When we last met Jonathan, he was taking action on his development plan. Jonathan will now walk through his worksheets and journal entries for embedding change systematically.

PERSONAL TRANSFORMATION ACTIVITY/PRACTICE LOG - JONATHAN'S EXAMPLE

Goal	Action	Record Actual Performance	Expected Impact	Priority	Measure	Progress	Feedback From Whom
Top 1	1. Let go of insignificant things 2. Manage the important details more effectively		Focus my time and energy on the right things at the right times, resulting in positive results without consequences	1	Reduction of unnecessary stress and level of necessary focus	Met goal 3x this week	My family members (parents and two brothers), and my professional /personal mentors
Top 2	Be able to work on and manage multiple projects at the same time		Increase my capacity to manage multiple projects at the same time, all of them working toward a common endpoint	2	Number and quality of projects that are working synchronously toward organizational goals	My personal/ professional mentors My colleagues	My personal/ professional mentors My colleagues
Top 3	4.						
	5.						
	6.						
Top 4	7.						
	8.						
	9.						

Innovative Leadership Reflection Questions

To help you develop your action plan, it is time to further clarify your direction using reflection questions. Questions for "What do I think/believe?" reflect your intentions. "What do I do?" questions reflect your actions. The questions "What do we believe?" reflect the culture of your organization (i.e., work, school, community), and "How do we do this?" questions reflect systems and processes for your organization. This exercise is an opportunity to practice innovative leadership by considering your vision for yourself and how it will play out in the context of your life. You will define your intentions, actions, culture, and systems in a systematic manner.

Table 8-2 contains an extensive list of questions to appeal to a broad range of readers. You will likely find a few of these questions fit your own personal situation; focus on the ones that seem most relevant. We recommend you answer one to three questions from each of the categories.

TABLE 8-2: QUESTIONS TO GUIDE THE LEADER AND ORGANIZATION

What do I think/ believe?

- How do I honor the progress I have made while maintaining focus on the balance of the work that needs to be done?
- How do I deal with both profound progress and a need for continued change?
- How do I deal with unresolved issues and uncertainty as I move forward?
- How do I deal with my desire to fix this issue and get back to the "real work?"
- What progress have I made as a leader/person?
- Are my assumptions still valid?
- As I have changed, am I still in the right role for my personal values and mission?
- How do I define myself as a leader? How do I think about my role and impact? How does my story about my effectiveness support or hinder my continued success?
- How does my belief about myself differ from how others see me?
- Am I still committed to the practices I developed?
- Am I willing to make these practices part of my life long-term?

What do I do?

- What do I communicate that conveys both progress and continued urgency?
- Am I visibly doing what I have committed to doing?
- Am I living up to the standards I have set for myself?
- Am I perceived as acting with integrity with regard to meeting my commitments?
- What do I do that reinforces the impact of my personal development?
- What do I do to sustain my new practices and development?
- How am I continuing to show the new behaviors I have publicly and privately committed to?
- How do I continue to sustain the practices I have started and the behavioral changes I have made? Have these changes become part of who I am, or will I slowly slide back to old behaviors—especially under stress or as other priorities emerge?
- Do I surround myself with others who are focused on their personal changes so that I have a reinforcement system?
- Do I continue to track and measure my progress?

What do we believe?

- What do we believe about people who are always focused on their development?
- What do we believe about ongoing development practices versus fixing problems then moving on?
- What do we believe about how to monitor and build momentum in different areas of life?
- What do we believe about appropriate pace and focus on development and growth?
- How do our beliefs about growth impact our ability to maintain momentum?

- What recognition is appropriate from different groups in my life (family, work, etc.)?

- How do we see ourselves now? How has our image of ourselves changed based on my personal change?

- Will the organization's goals and values change based on my personal changes?

- How do we react to old behaviors that no longer support the organization?

- If our organizational stories change about who we are, when do we incorporate new jargon, best practices, and human interest into emerging organizational stories?

How do we do this?
- What are the top three new behaviors others can expect to see? How will these behaviors be measured and reinforced?

- Who will remind me when I am struggling that I can make these changes?

- Do I clearly understand how my personal changes impact my work? Have I started to change the way I do my job? If my changes have an impact on how we interact, have we agreed on the new way we will work together?

- Do we need training to support new behaviors or interactions?

- What happens if I am not successful in meeting my top three goals? How would I like others to reinforce and/or support my behavioral changes?

- Do we have systems in place that discourage me from successfully accomplishing my top three goals?

- What processes/measures will we establish to identify behaviors that are no longer appropriate or necessary? What can I stop doing that will give me more time to practice?

- Are there any new ways to gain additional momentum to leverage existing changes and/or small wins?

- Am I reviewing measures regularly and recognizing results toward my change goals?

- Does the organization acknowledge people who have made changes (job starts and stops) and mastered new skills? Am I being rewarded for my personal development in this system?

- Do we continue to measure and reward actions that are necessary to sustain the changes using the updated job descriptions and process metrics? Am I still a good fit within this system?

- Has the organization rewarded me with recognition, promotion, increased responsibilities, or financial rewards?

Demetrius's Reflection Question Responses

We will now walk through Demetrius's answers to one or two questions from each section of Table 8-2.

What do I think/believe?

- *How do I honor the progress I have made while maintaining focus on the balance of the work that needs to be done?*

  Whenever my team is working on a project, I believe in rewarding the small victories as we move through our projects. I have taken the same approach in my personal progress. When it comes to my health, if I maintain my goals throughout the month, I reward myself with a new outfit in recognition of my effort. When I achieve my goal of thinking before responding to disagreeable information, it helps me to maintain a clearer head at work and enables me to deal with difficult situations that may come my way. With a clear mind, a healthy body, and emotions in check, I am much more equipped to balance the work that needs to be done.

- *What progress have I made as a leader/person? Are my assumptions still valid?*

I believe I have made significant progress toward becoming more conscious of my behaviors and practices, and how they impact my intentions. This has helped in my interactions with my team, colleagues, friends, and spouse. As I make these changes, I am seeing that my assumptions are still valid and that my direction is still the appropriate one for me.

I am committed to turning the actions in my plan into ongoing life practices. I can see that I am much more effective as a person and as a leader when I make time to care for myself and include balance and structure in sleep, diet, and exercise. I am also more compassionate and easier to work with when I take the time to consider problems and opportunities from many different perspectives, including the perspective of the person I may think is causing me the problem.

What do I do?

- *Am I living up to the standards I have set for myself?*

For the set of standards I have at this moment, I am absolutely living up to them. I also believe in reviewing and refining as I see appropriate. If I notice a standard is out of line with my beliefs, then it may be necessary to alter either a standard or belief to bring them into alignment.

- *Do I continue to track and measure my progress?*

I constantly check in with my support team to obtain their feedback about my progress toward my current goals. As a self-measure, I also keep a journal to better understand if I'm maintaining alignment. If I find that I'm veering off track, I take the necessary steps to get back on.

What do we believe?

- *What do we believe about people who are always focused on their development?*

As a leader, I am thrilled when members of my staff are focused on their development because as a leader my primary purpose is to help our people grow if that is their intent. With this focus, I'm sure people are also able to transfer some of their development the work they are currently performing—consequently, creating a win for them and a win for the organization.

■ *What do we believe about ongoing development practices versus fixing problems then moving on?*

I have come to believe that ongoing developmental practices greatly reduce the occurrence of—and, therefore, the need to fix—problems. Ongoing development allows us to continue to learn, to avoid potential detrimental issues, and to rely on and support each other's progress to meet our organization's goals.

How do we do this?

■ *Who will remind me when I am struggling that I can make the changes?*

I have mentioned this before and it's worth mentioning again: my wife is one of my biggest supporters. Whenever I am in a situation in which I find myself struggling, I know I can count on her to help, regardless of the circumstances. When I have thought about changing careers she has been there, when I have thought about changing jobs she has been there, so I have no reason to believe that her support will be any different moving forward.

■ *Do we need training to support new behaviors or interactions?*

As we talk more about leadership within the organization, I believe an assessment and high-level training from an external source would be beneficial for the firm.

Jonathan's Reflection Question Responses

We will now walk through Jonathan's answers to one or two questions from each section of Table 8-2.

What do I think/believe?

■ *How do I deal with my desire to fix this issue and get back to the "real work?"*

I make personal development an important piece of the "real work" on a daily basis. In order to fully invest myself in the personal development process, I need to view it as work and take time during my work day to focus in on it. I have to view my tangible outcomes at work and my outcomes in personal development as equally important outcomes.

What do I do?

■ *Do I surround myself with others who are focused on their personal changes so that I have a reinforcement system?*

I always surround myself with people who are committed to personal development, both within and outside of my organization, and this creates a culture of highly supportive personal development. Being around others who are disciplined to change keeps me accountable and motivated to make the personal change which I have laid out.

What do we believe?

- *What recognition is appropriate from different groups in my life (family, work)?*

  Different groups of people are differently disposed to give different types of feedback and recognition. My colleagues at work, for example, tend to recognize personal growth that results in organizational accomplishments. My family members, on the other hand, are able to more quickly recognize personal growth that results in personal and professional accomplishments.

How do we do this?

- *What can I stop doing that will give me more time to practice?*

  I can stop judging success by only the criteria of project execution and organizational progress, and start thinking about my personal development as a key criterion of success. This also helps me to view the personal development of my colleagues as an indicator of success. This cumulative personal development within our organization is a strong contributor to our organizational success in the long term.

Embed Innovation Systematically

Now that you have seen the worksheets and read through the sample narratives, it is time to complete the worksheets and answer the questions for yourself. We encourage you to complete all of the exercises and answer one to three reflection questions from each section in Table 8-2. This process serves to help you clarify what your barriers to success are and how you will manage or remove them.

In summary, this chapter helped you create an action plan and conduct thought experiments needed to sustain the changes you have invested so much time to generate. At this time in history, we culturally reinforce the idea of lifestyle changes like diet and exercise. This is also true of leadership development, awareness, and skill building. To sustain the changes you have made and continue to build on them, it is important for you to continually approach them with deliberation and a sense of presence.

In our dynamic environment, growth and development are required to stay relevant. This is perhaps more true now than at any other time in history, when growth is now a requirement to achieve and maintain success. Leadership growth is not only a matter of conceptual and pragmatic learning, but, also, about being introspective in our relationship with ourselves and with others.

What do I think/believe?

What do I do?

What do we believe?

How do we do this?

How will you and your support team celebrate your success?

Conclusion

Congratulations! If you started with the first step, you have finished the innovative leadership development process, and we trust you have seen a significant increase in your professional and personal effectiveness. It is time to celebrate your successes and the support you received from others! How will you acknowledge what you have accomplished? Consider reviewing your vision and SWOT analysis, and write down what you have accomplished.

How will you acknowledge the support others provided? How, in your culture, do you show gratitude and appreciation? When will you celebrate with your support team, either individually or collectively? Have you already been celebrating?

What Is Next For You?

Throughout this workbook, we provided a framework for developing innovative leadership to support your success. We augmented the process with a series of reflection questions and templates that can serve as guides. Based on our work with several hundred clients, we offer this specific combination of tools and framework to create a comprehensive approach that will allow you, the leader, to define what you want to change and give you a road map to support your development.

We provided Demetrius and Jonathan's stories to illustrate how to use the development process from an emerging leader perspective. By using the tools in the book and answering the questions about how an emerging leader would engage in development, Demetrius and Jonathan share the practical application of this theory with you.

Now that you have completed the workbook and established a solid personal development practice, it is time to think about whether you want to enhance your practice and begin the process again. Do you want to build on what you have created and revisit parts of the workbook that may be valuable at this time? You could start from the beginning and confirm your vision and values. Future iterations will likely take less time, as you now have experience with the development process. You may find that you focus on different areas based on your growth.

Congratulations on the progress you have made on your journey toward innovative leadership.

Enjoy your success!

References

Brown, Barrett. Conscious Leadership for Sustainability: How Leaders with Late-Stage Action Logic Design and Engage in Sustainability Initiatives. Ph.D. diss., Fielding Graduate University, 2011.

Collins, Jim. *Good to Great: Why some Companies Make the Leap… and Others Don't*. New York: HarperCollins Publishers, Inc., 2001.

Cook-Greuter, Susanne. *"A Detailed Description of Nine Action Logics in the Leadership Development Framework Adapted from Leadership Development Theory,"* www.cook-greuter.com, 2002.

Csikszentihalyi, Mihaly. *Flow: The Psychology of Optimal Experience*. New York: Harper Perennial, 1990.

Fitch, Geoff, Venita Ramirez, and Terri O'Fallon. "Enacting Containers for Integral Transformative Development." Presented at Integral Theory Conference, July 2010.

Fritz, Robert. *Path of Least Resistance: Learning to Become the Creative Force in Your Own Life*. Toronto: Random House, 1984.

Gauthier, Alain. "Developing Generative Change Leaders Across Sectors: An Exploration of Integral Approaches," *Integral Leadership Review*, June 2008.

Goleman, Daniel. *Working with Emotional Intelligence*. New York: Bantam Books, 1998.

Goleman, Daniel, Richard E. Boyatzis, and Annie McKee, *Primal Leadership: Learning to Lead with Emotional Intelligence*. Boston: Harvard Business School Press, 2002.

Goleman, Daniel. *Emotional Intelligence*. New York: Bantam Books, 1995.

Heath, Chip and Dan Heath. *Switch: How to Change Things When Change Is Hard*. New York: Broadway Books, 2010.

Howe-Murphy, Roxanne. *Deep Coaching: Using the Enneagram as a Catalyst for Profound Change,* El Granada: Enneagram Press, 2007.

Johnson, Barry. *Polarity Management: Identifying and Managing Unsolvable Problems*. Amherst: HRD Press, 1992.

Kegan, Robert and Lisa Laskow Lahey. *How the Way We Talk Can Change the Way We Work: Seven Languages for Transformation*. San Francisco: Jossey-Bass, 2001.

Klatt, Maryanna, Janet Buckworth, and William B. Malarkey. "Effects of Low-Dose Mindfulness-Based Stress Reduction (MBSR-ld) on Working Adults." Health Education and Behavior. Vol. 36, no. 3. 2009: 601-614.

Leonard, George and Michael Murphy. *The Life We Were Given: A Long Term Program for Realizing Potential of Body, Mind, Heart and Soul*. New York: Tarcher/Putnam, 1995.

Maddi, Salvatore R. and Deborah M. Khoshaba. *Resilience at Work: How to Succeed No Matter What Life Throws at You*. New York: MJF Books, 2005.

Metcalf, Maureen. "Level 5 Leadership: Leadership that Transforms Organizations and Creates Sustainable Results." *Integral Leadership Review,* March 2008.

Metcalf, Maureen, John Forman, and Dena Paluck. "Implementing Sustainable Transformation – Theory and Application." *Integral Leadership Review,* June 2008.

Metcalf, Maureen and Dena Paluck. "The Story of Jill: How an Individual Leader Developed into a 'Level 5' Leader." *Integral Leadership Review,* June 2010.

Northouse, Peter G. *Leadership: Theory and Practice.* Thousand Oaks: Sage Publications, 2010.

O'Fallon, Terri, Venita Ramirez, Jesse McKay, and Kari Mays. "Collective Individualism: Experiments in Second Tier Community." Presented at Integral Theory Conference, August 2008.

O'Fallon, Terri. "The Collapse of the Wilber-Combs Matrix: The Interpenetration of the State and Structure Stages." Presented at Integral Theory Conference, July 2010 (1st place winner).

O'Fallon, Terri. "Integral Leadership Development: Overview of our Leadership Development Approach." www.pacificintegral.com, 2011.

Patterson, Kerry, Joseph Grenny, Ron McMillan, and Al Switzler. *Crucial Conversations: Tools for talking when stakes are high.* New York: McGraw-Hill, 2002.

Richmer, Hilke R. An Analysis of the Effects Of Enneagram-Based Leader Development On Self-Awareness: A Case Study at a Midwest Utility Company. Ph.D. diss., Spalding University, 2011.

Riso, Don Richard, and Russ Hudson. *The Wisdom of the Enneagram: The Complete Guide to Psychological and Spiritual Growth for the Nine Personality Types.* New York: Bantam, 1999.

Riso, Don Richard and Russ Hudson. *Personality Types: Using the Enneagram for Self-Discovery.* New York: Houghton Mifflin, 1996.

Rooke, David and William R. Torbert. "Seven Transformations of Leadership," *Harvard Business Review,* April 2005.

Rooke, David and William R. Torbert. "Organizational Transformation as a Function of CEOs' Developmental Stage." *Organization Development Journal* 16, 1, 1998: 11-28.

Senge, Peter, Art Kleiner, Charlotte Roberts, Richard Ross, and Bryan Smith. *The Fifth Discipline Fieldbook: Strategies and Tools for Building a Learning Organization.* New York: Doubleday, 1994.

Torbert, William R. and Associates. *Action Inquiry: The Secret of Timely and Transforming Leadership.* San Francisco: Berrett-Koehler Publishing, Inc., 2004.

Wigglesworth, Cindy. "Why Spiritual Intelligence Is Essential to Mature Leadership," *Integral Leadership Review,* August 2006.

Wilber, Ken. "Introduction to Integral Theory and Practice: IOS Basic and AQAL Map." www.integralnaked.org.

Author Bio

Maureen Metcalf

Maureen is the founder and CEO of Metcalf & Associates, Inc., a management consulting and coaching firm dedicated to helping leaders, their management teams and organizations implement the innovative leadership practices necessary to thrive in a rapidly changing environment.

Maureen is an acclaimed thought leader who developed, tested, and implemented emerging models that dramatically improve leaders and organizations success in changing times. She works with leaders to develop innovative leadership capacity and with organizations to further develop innovative leadership qualities. Maureen is at the forefront of helping organizations to explore these emerging solutions for long-term organizational sustainability.

As a senior manager with two "Big Four" Management consulting firms for 12 years, Maureen managed and contributed to successful completion of a wide array of projects from strategy development and organizational design for start-up companies to large system change for well-established organizations. She has worked with a number of Fortune 100 clients delivering a wide range of significant business results such as: increased profitability, cycle time reduction, increased employee engagement and effectiveness, and improved quality.

Thank you for reading!

Thank you for taking the time to read the Innovative Leadership Workbook for Emerging Leaders and Managers.

I trust the worksheets and reflection questions you completed here will help you become a more effective leader. Because growth has a ripple effect dynamic, we welcome your suggestions, additional tools and templates. Please contact me at:

>Maureen Metcalf
>Metcalf & Associates, Inc.
>Maureen@metcalf-associates.com

This is the third in a series of workbooks. Subsequent workbooks will be written for public service executives and more. Download other titles on Innovative Leadership at www.innovativeleadershipfieldbook.com.

CPSIA information can be obtained at www.ICGtesting.com
Printed in the USA
BVOW06s1105110315

391249BV00019B/249/P